THE PENGUIN CLASSICS

FOUNDER EDITOR (1944–64): E. V. RIEU

Editor: Betty Radice

Mother Julian of Norwich was born towards the end of 1342; the date of her death is unknown, but she probably lived well into her seventies, being made the beneficiary of a will in 1416. The sixteen unforgettable revelations or 'shewings' which she recounts in this book were experienced on 8 May 1373 following an illness, when it is believed she was still living in her mother's house. At what stage in her life she became an anchoress is not clear, but she was certainly a 'recluse atte Norwyche' by 1400, being supported in a cell by the church of St Julian and St Edward at Conisford (itself attached to the Benedictine Community at Carrow). Her fame as a spiritual counsellor was widespread, and though she describes herself as 'a simple creature unlettyrde' she was clearly a woman of keen intellect, learning and integrity.

CLIFTON WOLTERS was born in London, and trained for the priesthood at Durham University and the London College of Divinity. He was Vicar of Wimbledon Park, and later Rector of Sanderstead. He is now Provost of Newcastle. He has also translated *The Cloud of Unknowing* and Richard Rolle's *Fire of Love* for the Penguin Classics.

JULIAN OF NORWICH

Revelations of Divine Love

TRANSLATED INTO MODERN ENGLISH
AND WITH AN INTRODUCTION BY

CLIFTON WOLTERS

PENGUIN BOOKS

Penguin Books Ltd, Harmondsworth, Middlesex, England
Penguin Books, 625 Madison Avenue, New York, New York 10022, U.S.A.
Penguin Books Australia Ltd, Ringwood, Victoria, Australia
Penguin Books Canada Ltd, 2801 John Street, Markham, Ontario, Canada L3R 1B4
Penguin Books (N.Z.) Ltd, 182–190 Wairau Road, Auckland 10, New Zealand

—

This translation first published 1966
Reprinted 1973, 1974, 1976, 1978, 1980

—

—

Made and printed in Great Britain
by Richard Clay (The Chaucer Press) Ltd,
Bungay, Suffolk
Set in Monotype Bembo

JOHANNI, FILIO MEO,
AMICO ET FRATRI

CONTENTS

Introduction

Revelations of Divine Love

Introduction

The Church and Revelations

'SIR, the pretending to extraordinary revelations and gifts of the Holy Ghost is a horrid thing, a very horrid thing,' said Bishop Butler to John Wesley. St Paul shared the bishop's disquiet, albeit more philosophically. 'How is it then, brethren,' he writes to his converts at Corinth, 'when ye come together every one of you hath . . . a revelation?' One can still catch the hint of exasperation in his voice.

The Church has always tended to react negatively to 'revelations', and sensible men everywhere will applaud such hesitance. But not to *all* revelations, for a body which professes belief in the living and self-revealing God has by that very fact to admit the possibility of his communicating with his people whenever he chooses, in the first century or now. Neither the bishop nor his predecessor would gainsay this; nor would they be any less wary.

Religion knows many stories of people who have claimed special revelations of divine truth, and who have been patently wrong. They were not necessarily mad. But the genuineness of a revelation is not so much dependent on the opinion of the recipient as on the content of its subject matter, and from the first the Church has 'tried the spirits whether they were of God'. In the process of time she has acquired considerable skill in this matter.

No rule of thumb is adequate in affairs of such delicacy, nor, on the other hand, can a hard-and-fast formula be infallible. In general, the theologians apply a series of tests, and only if the presumed revelation passes them all may it be regarded as being of divine inspiration; and then, normally, it is looked upon as having value only for the visionary himself.

One would like to think that the good faith of the seer

could be taken for granted, but experience suggests that this is not always so. On the principle that safety is better than sorrow, a careful inquiry is always made into such matters as his general integrity and character, his health of mind and body, his education and domestic background. A similar probe is made into his spiritual capacity in order to assess, for example, the reality of his goodness and the depth of his humility, his willingness to submit to expert guidance and the quality of his piety. None of these factors is unimportant in coming to a decision. Moreover, the truth or otherwise of the revelation will be reflected in the after-effects, and the omens are reckoned to be favourable if there is a heightening of piety, peace, poise, penitence, and patience, and, above all, the desire to do only what pleases God.

Even so 'The end is not yet', for there are further hurdles to negotiate. Does the revelation accord with the teaching of the Church? Does it commend itself to Christian reason? Is there some other explanation? If the results of all these tests are positive it is *probable* that there has been a genuine revelation. Yet the pundits hesitate. They will say that the vision is primarily the concern of the recipient; perhaps it may be communicated to others for their edification and instruction, and even be thought worthy of publication, but on no account is it to be regarded as a substitute for the dogmatic teaching of the Church, be it never so helpful and true to the receiver. Nor should a repeat of the experience be sought for – for that is God's business and no one else's. One cannot even be sure that what has been described has been described accurately, for in the nature of things a divine vision is fundamentally indescribable. And no amount of bona fide revelations will mark a man as any holier than any other; most Christians do not need such things. The theologians do not thrill when the prophet cries, 'Thus saith the Lord!' They first examine his credentials.

One need not be too cynical about this lack of enthusiasm. The questions are, after all, only those that sanctified common sense must always ask. Perhaps they are more formidable on paper than in reality. The continuing fact is that few revelations survive this screening, and of those that do, not all deserve publishing.

The *Revelations of Divine Love* by Mother Julian were recognized from the first to have more than a private and personal value, a judgement that each reader may test for himself if he will read her vivid and strangely moving record with due sympathy. It is not the purpose of this introduction to 'grill' Julian in the terms of what has been written above. She is her own best defence, and needs not that we should protect her.

Two Versions

Her book has come down to us in two versions, one being considerably longer than the other. Of the longer version three manuscripts are known to exist, two in the British Museum (MS. Sloane 2499 and MS. Sloane 3705), and one in the Bibliothèque Nationale, Paris (No 40 Fonds Anglais). Of the British Museum manuscripts, Sloane 2499 appears to date from the middle of the seventeenth century, and Sloane 3705 from the end of the same century or early in the next. The Paris manuscript is the earliest and dates from the sixteenth century.

Only one copy of the shorter version exists, and that is in an omnibus book of medieval devotion, bought by the British Museum in 1909 from Lord Amherst (MSS. Additional 37790). In some cases the examples of this Middle Age piety consist of extracts from longer works, and it is a plausible suggestion that its version of Mother Julian is a digest of the longer one, for it is only a third of its length. But scholars are not willing to accept this. They argue that the shorter account is the original one made by Julian soon after the visions were received, and that the longer version is built upon it, enriched by the fruits of twenty years' brooding. In support they point out that there is not the least trace of the shorter version's having been a summary; that it contains in embryo all that is discussed at much greater length in the long version – in other words, that it was intended as a basis for subsequent meditation, and therefore merely a first transcript; and that the graphic and circumstantial details of an earlier account would, with the passage of time, lose value in Julian's eyes – dwelling on the eternal mysteries, she would instinctively tend to omit the 'frills'. Such reasoning carries its own conviction.

This present translation is made from the longer, expanded version, and is based on Sloane 2499, generally accepted as the most reliable of the extant versions.

The Writer

Most of our knowledge of Julian comes from the autobiographical details in the two versions of her vision, and it might well be wished that they were more. There are a few contemporary references to her, which do not add up to very much, and it has to be admitted that as an historical figure little is known about her; of her as a person, however, her book reveals considerably more.

She writes that the revelations were given in May 1373, when she was thirty and a half years old, which must mean that she was born towards the end of 1342. Later, in the longer version of her experiences, she recalls that she had been brooding on them for almost twenty years (Chapter

51), so she was alive in 1393. Evidence from three wills names her as a beneficiary, and as the latest of these is dated 1416, it is not unreasonable to think that she was still living in that year, now well on in her seventies. It is these wills, as well as unvarying tradition, which make it plain that she was a 'recluse atte Norwyche', and that the church that supported her anchorage was St Julian and St Edward's, Conisford. The church itself belonged to the Benedictine Community at Carrow.

It cannot be said with any certainty that she was a solitary in 1373. Her mother was in attendance, together with other companions, at the illness from which she nearly died, and which was the context of the revelations. The parish priest who came to administer the last rites was accompanied by a child. Even when allowance is made for the comparative liberty of a medieval anchorhold, the numbers and nature of those present at her putative dying would seem to indicate that she was not enclosed at that time. Yet a hint ('This place is a prison' – Chapter 77) may refer to her manner of life when she was writing the longer version, and could mean therefore that she was a recluse by then. It might not be too wide of the mark to assume that these revelations were granted to a deeply religious woman still living at home, who as a result of them retired into a more perfect way of life – as her contemporaries would see it – as an anchoress. But this is conjecture, not proven fact: no one knows. Neither is it known whether she was ever a professed nun. The link of her cell with the Benedictine Community at Carrow suggests the possibility, for it was usual though not universal for anchorages to be occupied by members of the holding body, as is still the case. There is nothing peculiarly Benedictine about Julian's book to make the identification certain. The fact that she is variously described as 'Dame', 'Lady', and 'Mother', does not help in this respect, for such titles were ascribed indiscriminately to anchoresses and the fully professed. The most interesting and extensive contemporary reference to her comes from that queer, unbalanced creature, Margery Kempe. It is vivid enough to be quoted in full:

Then she was bidden by Our Lord to go to an anchoress in the same city, named Dame Jelyan, [i.e. Julian – Ed.] and so she did, and showed her the grace that God put into her soul, of compunction, contrition, sweetness and devotion, compassion with holy meditation and high contemplation, and fully many holy speeches and dalliance that Our Lord spoke to her soul; and many wonderful revelations, which she showed to the anchoress to find out if there were any deceit in them, for the anchoress was expert in such things, and good counsel could give.

The anchoress, hearing the marvellous goodness of Our Lord, highly thanked God with all her heart for his visitation, counselling this creature to be obedient to the will of Our Lord God and to fulfil with all her might whatever he put into her soul, if it were not against the worship of God and profit of her fellow Christians, for if it were, then it were not the moving of a good spirit, but rather of an evil spirit. 'The Holy Ghost moveth ne'er a thing against charity, for if he did, he would be contrary to his own self for he is all charity. Also he moveth a soul to all chasteness, for chaste livers are called the temple of the Holy Ghost, and the Holy Ghost maketh a soul stable and steadfast in the right faith, and the right belief.

'And a double man in soul is ever unstable and unsteadfast in all his ways. He that is ever doubting is like the flood of the sea which is moved and borne about with the wind, and that man is not likely to receive the gifts of God.

'Any creature that hath these tokens may steadfastly believe that the Holy Ghost dwells in his soul. And much more when God visiteth a creature with tears of contrition, devotion and compassion, he may and ought to believe that the Holy Ghost is in his soul. Saint Paul saith that the Holy Ghost asketh for us with mourning and weeping unspeakable, that is to say, he maketh us to ask and pray with mourning and weeping so plenteously that the tears may not be numbered. No evil spirit may give these tokens, for Saint Jerome saith that tears torment more the devil than do the pains of hell. God and the devil are ever at odds and they shall never dwell together in one place, and the devil hath no power in a man's soul.

'Holy Writ saith that the soul of a rightful man is the sea lof God, and so I trust, sister, that ye be. I pray God grant you perseverance. Set all your trust in God and fear not the language of the world, for the more despite, shame and reproof that ye have in the world, the more is your merit in the sight of God. Patience is necessary to you, for in that ye shall keep your soul.'

Much was the holy dalliance that the anchoress and this creature had by communing in the love of Our Lord Jesus Christ the many days that they were together.*

Her Sources and Style

Julian makes a modest and characteristic disclaimer of her literary ability. She calls herself 'unlettered' (Chapter 2), which with the evidence before us is palpably untrue. Both her book, and Margery Kempe's account of the interview, show her to be a sympathetic, shrewd, and learned person, with her feet very much on the ground. But the belittling adjective may mean no more than that at the time of the showings she could not read – a defect that was corrected later – or, more probably, that she had no skill in church Latin. Some substance for this latter interpretation may be found in her not wholly orthodox 'Benedicite Domine' of Chapter 4. If this is not a copyist's error, it might be Julian's. Scholarly heads have been shaken over this.

There is not much to be gained from discussing her literary

* *Book of Margery Kempe*, quoted by permission of the Editor, W. Butler-Bowdon, and Oxford University Press, 1954; pages 54–6.

sources. Whatever they were, by the time she wrote she had so assimilated them that they were part and parcel of her thinking. One is reduced virtually to guessing, and tracing similarities. But there are two sources identified and identifiable, the Bible and Pseudo-Dionysius.* The Scriptures she quotes frequently, and not always accurately; yet they colour her whole outlook, and the occasional lapses only serve to emphasize this fact. 'Saint Dionyse of France', as she mistakenly calls the Areopagite, was her other influence, but it is difficult to know whether she had read his *Hid Divinite* and other works, or had merely absorbed his teaching from the common mystical heritage of her day. Certainly she makes use of Dionysian words and thoughts, though she parts company with him when she deals with the problem of evil. And the general trend of her thought is much more positive and optimistic than his. If she had read Pseudo-Dionysius at all, she had read him critically and selectively.

It can be assumed that she would know the *Ancrene Riwle*,

* Dionysius the Areopagite was one of St Paul's converts at Athens (Acts xvii, 34). Nothing more is known of him, but for a thousand years or so he was believed to be the author of a group of mystical writings which were immensely influential in the formation of Christian spirituality. The actual author is thought to be an unnamed Syrian monk of the early sixth century, who sought to further his teaching by a false ascription of authorship. Among the writings which survive are the *Celestial Hierarchy*, the *Ecclesiastical Hierarchy*, the *Divine Names*, and the *Mystical Theology*, the last one of which was put into English by the writer of *The Cloud of Unknowing* under the title of *Hid Divinite*. It was not until the sixteenth century that the Dionysian origin began to be doubted, and it was much longer before it was universally regarded as Pseudo. To put a wrong maker's label on the jar is today properly regarded as a crime, though it does not necessarily affect the quality of the jam. In the early centuries of the Church it was a common and accepted practice, designed to stress the soundness of the contents. *Autres temps, autres mœurs*. At the time that Julian was writing, the Church firmly believed in the quasi-apostolic authority of St Dionysius.

the thirteenth-century Rule for Anchoresses, for this guide book was almost *de rigueur* for the medieval solitary. Possibly, too, she might know something of *St Augustine*, for in the same street as her anchorage was an Augustinian friary. Her many references to the grace of God could be as much due to this contact as to the general reaction of conservative churchmen to the teachings of William of Ockham. *St Gregory* provides the only direct non-scriptural quotation. It comes from his *Life of Saint Benedict*, and does little more than raise the question whether she was a nun before reclusion. It does not even demonstrate that she was a Gregorian devotee. Of a knowledge of contemporary mystical literature there is little sign, although there are passages in the works of Walter Hilton which could have inspired, or have been inspired by, Julian, so similar are they. At this distance of time, and with no supporting evidence, no one can say who influenced whom.

Her literary style is spontaneous and unaffected. There is a vividness about her reporting which communicates itself to the reader and carries him along. She has an eye for detail and, perhaps because she is a woman, for colour and clothes. There is a natural ability to turn a phrase, and one sometimes wonders if her balanced and rhetorical sentences owe anything to the occasional sermon she would have heard as well as to the books she would have read. Such tricks of speech were fashionable in her day, as was the fondness for alliteration that she sometimes indulges. Her vocabulary is a tolerably wide one, with a certain predilection for words of Latin or French derivation. Her English is a blend of East Anglian and Northern dialects.

Theologically, Julian's language and style are accurate and precise, whether she is dealing with dogma or spirituality. There is no sign of her being untutored here. Yet she is never fussy or pedantic, and it is likely that her great flair for putting profundities into simple terms saves her from this not unknown failing. The reader will note her determination always to submit her experiences and her interpretations to the judgement of Holy Church, and her clear intention to be wholly orthodox. Yet he will also sense the power of her vigorous intellect, and a certain independence of thought which periodically she has to restrain. Further reflection may suggest that this woman's piety, so skilfully presented, was extremely comprehensive and balanced. Faith, vision, creed, prayer, mystical union, sacrament, and even the ecclesiastical set-up, are all part of the spiritual life, combining without clashing to build up the soul in God. She is an honest, obedient, and integrated person – and her writing reflects it. Yet when all this has been said it must be confessed that she can at times be very involved and obscure. There are paragraphs and sentences that could be pruned radically without loss and given a sharper edge. It is true that translators take the occasional liberty when seeking to put an author into contemporary language, but to do so here in these turgid passages would seem to the present Editor to confuse freedom with licence. And so he has sought to translate 'warts and all', while he remembers that there may be other obscurities in this text which are not so much due to Julian as to her modernizer. Very rarely do works improve by being translated. Julian is more obscure than is generally recognized. Perhaps this is due to the sort of gold-panning treatment she is subjected to by those on the look out for nuggets. Golden sentences there are in plenty, but in the process of isolating them a lot of very rich minerals are sieved away. It is more profitable to treat her as a coal mine and work the seams. The yield is greater and more rewarding.

The Recluse atte Norwyche

In these days of collective thinking the individualism of the religious and solitary life is found by many to be somewhat embarrassing. Withdrawal from the world in order to give oneself to prayer is thought to be selfish and cowardly, and strong pressures of dissuasion are brought to bear on those who fancy themselves called to a life of reclusion. Popular opinion neither understands nor approves. Despite this general attitude, men and women do leave the world, not only to become monks or nuns but to embrace the solitary life as well. The contemplative Orders, Anglican and Roman, are experiencing a quiet boom in vocations, and the number of religious recluses, admittedly small, increases rather than decreases. Publicity could ruin everything, and therefore, little is given.

Times have changed. In the Middle Ages the solitary life was almost popular. It took various forms. There were *hermits*, foot-loose male solitaries who retained a considerable freedom of movement, changing from one place to another according to circumstances. Their 'good works' often expressed themselves in the servicing of roads and bridges. A *recluse* was one who was shut away from normal social life. It is a loose description of a hermit, but is more accurately a synonym for the *anchorite* (m.)* or *anchoress* (f.), who were enclosed in their anchorages (cf. vicarage, parsonage), living on their anchorhold, primarily to engage in a life of sacrifice and prayer.

Every town of any consequence sought to have at least one solitary, and often made a substantial contribution by way of maintenance. 'They were regarded as part of its welfare

* Both hermit and anchorite are words of Greek origin; cf. eremites = one who dwells in the desert; anachoreo = I withdraw.

services,' writes Peter Anson, 'quite worth maintaining for the spiritual good derived from their prayers and penances.'*
There is a touch of picturesque exaggeration here, but sufficient traces of anchorholds have survived the ravages of the Reformation to show how many there must have been in this country alone. It is worthy of note that, in that wonderful fourteenth century when English mysticism burst into flower, the four great masters were either solitaries themselves or else writing for them. Mother Julian was one such; the author of *The Cloud of Unknowing* wrote for a young intending recluse; Walter Hilton wrote his *Ladder of Perfection* for anchoresses; and Richard Rolle was a hermit.

The same period has been called the 'Golden Age of the English Recluse',† and has left sufficient account of itself to enable an accurate and comprehensive picture of the life to be drawn. From the records it is known, for example, that there were six recluses living in Winchester in 1259, two at Lincoln in 1392, eight (at least) in London about the same time. In 1415 Lord Scrope of Masham left benefactions to solitaries in 'London and York, with their suburbs; as well as the anchorets and recluses of Beverley, Stafford, Hampole, Leek, Newcastle, Gainsborough, Southwell, Stamford, Dartford, Shrewsbury, Kirkby Wath, Kexby Wighton', and three other places. There were anchorages in churches, monasteries, convents, and castles. Obviously there was no shortage of vocations.

When a man or woman believed himself to have been called to this life the normal procedure was to have his claim investigated by an officer appointed by the bishop of the diocese: it might be an archdeacon or an abbot. In addition, he had to show that he was able to sustain himself one way or

---

* Peter Anson, *The Call of the Desert* (see Bibliography), page 176.
† Francis D. S. Darwin, *The English Mediaeval Recluse* (see Bibliography), page 65.

another during his confinement. If he was able to satisfy his examiners on both these scores he would be enclosed in his cell, never to leave it again.

The service of enclosure was both spectacular and grim. Though it varied somewhat from diocese to diocese, in essentials it was the same. In the setting of the Mass – more generally, of the Dead, though sometimes of the Holy Spirit – the profession of the candidate was made, and his 'clothing' performed. At the conclusion, a procession was made from the church to the cell, while psalms or litanies were being sung. The cell was blessed and the new occupant sprinkled with holy water and censed. He was then invited to enter. This was to be his 'tomb', for from henceforth he must be considered as 'dead unto the world and alive unto God'. Here the various ceremonies of the Burial Office seem to have been enacted. Holy smoke and water, the prostration of the recluse upon the bier, the scattering of earth – nothing was left to the imagination; and at the end of it all, with the safe emergence of the bishop, 'let them block up the entrance to the house'.

It would be wrong to imagine that the cell was the tiny uncomfortable room of popular belief. It was unlikely to have been a mere bed-sitter. More probably it would have been a suite of several rooms, or even the medieval equivalent of a bungalow surrounded by its own fenced garden. There was no standard pattern. Indeed, some anchoresses lived together. The three sisters for whom the *Ancrene Riwle* was written lived in adjacent and communicating cells, with a couple of maids and a kitchen-boy to wait on them. There is frequent mention of 'servants' in the various records, and it is almost certain that few recluses would have experienced utter physical solitude all the time. From the evidence of contemporary wills it is known that Mother Julian had had at least two servants in her time, named Sara and Alice. They would do the necessary shopping and preserve the outside contacts without which no one can live. It was not unknown for these solitaries to have their own cattle, often a potential cause of scandal, but indicative of the comparative freedom of movement and outlook granted by medieval society to those religious. In England, if not elsewhere, there was no obligation to embrace Holy Poverty by renouncing all property or by refusing gifts. Rules with regard to clothing and food were sensible without being lavish. In some instances, there are accounts of staying guests having been entertained by the recluse; there was no proscription of visitors for the day. If all this is felt to be typical of the laxity of the Church before it was reformed, let it be remembered that the underlying facts remained unaltered: it was a life of prayer and self-denial, and with the rarest exceptions the anchorite was cell-bound till he died. Some ran away, of course; some went mad; the great majority were faithful unto physical death, thanks to the safety valve provided by this mitigated rule. Not all solitaries lived in this limited comfort however. There were those who survived conditions that were austere by any standard. But these seem to have been the exception: generally extremism was avoided, and sound sense prevailed.

What did they do? Fundamentally, they prayed: if they were in vows, according to Holy Rule; if they were seculars, according to the rule of their bishop; if they were priests, they would say Mass; if they were lay folk, they would assist thereat. The *Ancrene Riwle* provides a fairly tight schedule of prayers to be said at different times of the day, and this Rule had wide influence. Mother Julian cannot have been unique in the quality of the prayer life she lived: many another found that he was in fact alone with God, and was raised to great heights of prayer.

But though prayer was their primary function they did much else. It accorded with the skill and penchant of the individual. Embroidery and needlework and teaching little girls were usual among women, writing and illuminating and crafts generally were done by the men. Both men and women acted as spiritual directors or advisers, as Margery Kempe's visit to Mother Julian suggests. This, and the fact that they could always be approached through their world-side window, meant that gossip was an ever-present temptation, and frequent warnings against this particular form of sin can be found.

The Mystic

Ever since Dean Inge compiled his famous list of definitions,* 'mysticism' has been recognized as being susceptible of very many meanings. The situation today is not much improved on 1899, and the theologian makes comparatively little use of the word, preferring to stick to a vocabulary less ambiguous. For his own convenience he will divide the theology of spirituality into 'ascetical' and 'mystical', which latter adjective covers the advanced stages of the life of prayer. The Christian mystic is regarded as one who has been raised to a high degree of contemplative prayer. The mystical experience consists in a conscious, deep, and intimate union of the soul with God who has taken the initiative therefor; while the soul, on its part, has prepared itself, normally according to an accepted pattern of asceticism. This is no new thing, of course, but is part of the developed doctrine of prayer down the centuries, and in this sense 'mysticism' dates from New Testament times. What a curious public delights in as 'mystical phenomena' – levitations, ecstasies, trances, and the like – are unimportant. They are regarded as inessential, and as much a hindrance as a help. They prove nothing – not even the holiness of the entranced.

* In his Bampton Lectures on *Christian Mysticism* (Methuen, 1899).

Union with God is something which by its very nature cannot be fully described. God can never be measured by human minds, and intimacy with him exhausts and transcends the power of language and the range of thought. This fundamental limitation of our psychical faculties can produce confusion of mind, and even a sense of dereliction, in the soul's vain attempt to recapture the ineffable and the incommunicable. And, since a human being is body as well as soul and mind, it is not surprising that in the early stages of this kind of advanced prayer there can be physical reactions too; though it would seem that by-products of this sort are governed to a large extent by the temperament and character of the particular contemplative. But in nearly every case the memory of the first divine 'touch' persists, to haunt the recipient who longs for, while he dreads, another such visitation. If it comes, and comes again, the soul becomes more sensitive and able to deal with it, and the reactions of a puzzled mind and body are less worrying. But so much depends on the individual personality that one can never safely predict how or when these difficulties will vanish, and the consolations prevail, and God break through again.

Is Julian a mystic in the generally accepted sense of the word? The answer must be 'yes', for though her book is primarily concerned with the showings and her meditations on them, it is also its own witness that the manner of these visions was in itself mystical, and that in five brief hours Julian sampled most of the wide range of mystical experience. There were no observable phenomena in her case. The vision and the concomitant locutions were peculiar to herself and not to her companions.

But the problems of reclusion and mysticism have comparatively little influence on the value of her 'revelations', and it is with these that the rest of this simple introduction will be concerned.

The Showings

(a) Her reason for writing

The fourteenth and fifteenth centuries produced a whole crop of mystical writings purporting to be revelations received from God. The fact that nearly all the great visionaries were women suggests the possibility that there is something in the feminine make-up which renders it peculiarly sensitive to such visitations, whether imaginary or real. Whatever the psychological reason, however, Mother Julian does not seem to be aware that she is in the current fashion; indeed, more than once she apologizes for her gender as if she felt it to be a disadvantage when handling spiritual matters, and a factor militating against her competence. But she wrote because she felt compelled to do so; she had no doubt about the reality of her mystical experience, and she was anxious to share it with her 'even-Christians', not for her own glorification, but for their edification and pleasure. In several places she refers to the reasons for her writing, but nowhere more clearly than in Chapter 6 of the shorter version:

I know well this that I say – I have it on the showing of him who is a sovereign Teacher – and truly charity urgeth me to tell you of it, for I would that God were known and my fellow-Christians helped (as I would be myself), to the more hating of sin and loving of God. Because I am a woman should I therefore believe that I ought not to tell you about the goodness of God since I saw at the same time that it is his will that it be known?

(b) The occasion of the showings

On that unforgettable eighth of May 1373 – it was the third Sunday after Easter, and the day after the festival of St John of Beverley – she was already a woman of considerable spiritual maturity. Some time previously, and long enough ago for her to have forgotten all about it, she had asked a threefold favour of God which would enable her to serve him more fully and to know him more intimately. In her own words she sought this: 'The first was mind of his Passion; the second was bodily sickness in youth, at thirty years of age; the third was to have of God's gift three wounds' (Chapter 2). 'The cause of this' (the first) 'petition was that . . . I should have the more true mind in the Passion of Christ.' She would be of the company that watched by the Cross, and suffer with them and him. The second request was made in order that 'I might be purged, by the mercy of God, and afterward live more to the worship of God because of that sickness. And that for the more speed in my death: for I desired to be soon with my God.' Both these petitions were conditional upon their being consonant with God's will, and perhaps for that reason passed from her conscious memory. The third, however, 'dwelled with me continually'. It was 'a mighty desire to receive three wounds . . . the wound of very contrition, the wound of kind compassion, and the wound of wilful longing toward God. And all this last petition I asked without any condition' (Chapter 2).

Greatly to her surprise all three prayers were granted. At the beginning of that memorable month she was stricken with an unspecified illness of such gravity that she was thought to be dying, a belief that she herself fully shared. After a week her parish priest gave her the last rites, and as he left set a crucifix before her glazing eyes, bidding her look on the face of her Saviour and Creator, and comfort herself thereby. As she gave herself to such consideration she received these sixteen 'showings' or revelations, in fairly rapid succession. The first fifteen were, in fact, given in five hours, from four o'clock to nine, the morning following the clerical visit (Chapter 65). The sixteenth occurred during the ensuing night, as a sort of conclusion and confirmation of the others (Chapter 66).

(c) The integrity of the visions

Much speculation has been devoted to the nature of Julian's illness, and to the genuineness of the revelations of which it was the setting. This is not the place to do more than mention the whole discussion, and to summarize it by saying that scholars are for the most part willing to accept it as an actual physical sickness. They are agreed, moreover, that the evidence supports the claim that this rather down-to-earth and practical woman did receive insight into matters about which it is unlikely that she could have had informed and balanced views.

Despite the existence of two versions of different length it is not always possible to distinguish the original account from her later reflections. The shorter version is generally accepted as being the first transcript, written soon after the revelations were given. The longer one is confessedly written twenty years later (Chapter 51), and contains the fruits of much meditation upon that happening. Sometimes, though not very often, one wonders whether subsequent meditation has embroidered the pristine vision. It would be surprising if it had not.

Though in the last resort it must always be the subjective opinion of the reader which accepts or rejects the revelations as genuine, it is some guide to know that the Church as a whole is prepared to declare them a private revelation worthy of dissemination. Probably most who read with sympathy this straightforward narrative will concur with this judgement. When generous allowance has been made for the embellishments of twenty years' reflection, and her deprecatory 'unlettered' has been discounted, the sheer integrity of Julian's reasoning, the precision of her theology, the depth of her insight, and the simplicity with which she expounds profound truths, call for a satisfactory explanation. Only if one is going to deny any possibility of a divine communication can Julian's claim be completely ruled out. It is a reasonable hypothesis that her explanation could be true, basically if not in every detail.

(d) The threefold manner of her seeing

The 'showings' came to Julian in three ways.

All the blessed teaching of our Lord God was showed by three parts; that is to say, by bodily sight, and by word formed in my understanding, and by ghostly sight. For the 'bodily sight' I have said as I saw, as truly as I can. And for the 'words', I have said them right as our Lord showed them to me. And for the 'ghostly sight', I have said some deal, but I may never fully tell it.* [Chapter 73]

Julian's 'three parts' have been equated by some with the classical threefold division of visionary experience first made by St Augustine. This analysis was a godsend to the medieval theologian, for it provided a convenient description of the customary ways in which 'young men' (and women) 'saw visions, and old men dreamed dreams'. But like all these useful formulae it has tended to be regarded as a rule of universal application, and sometimes Julian has been dressed in clothes that do not fit her, and explained in ways less than just. St Augustine believed that some visions were 'corporeal'; that is, they were accepted by the seer as present in fact to his senses. Some were 'imaginary', seen (and recognized as such) in the mind of the percipient. And some were 'intellectual', being fed into the soul by the direct action of God. But this straight-jacket does not suit Julian, who, in blissful ignorance that the last word had been said by the greatest of the Latin Fathers, described her visions in her own fashion, and with her own

* B.M., M S. Sloane 2499 (spelling and punctuation modernized).

terminology. It is not always possible to maintain that Julian observes her distinctions consistently, for 'bodily sight' and 'ghostly in bodily likeness' and 'more ghostly without bodily likeness' and 'ghostly sight' occasionally overlap. This blurring matters little. The surprise is that she should be as sure-footed and precise as she is, when she seeks to describe what at its height is ineffable, and before which the vocabulary of the mystical theologian, much later evolved, stands confused and tongue-tied.

(e) Some characteristics of her teaching

(i) *God.* Like all true mystics Julian's prime concern is with God, and with man's relationship to him. Unlike some of her contemporaries (for example, the author of *The Cloud of Unknowing*) she insists on our constant recalling of God's self-revelation as Three in One. This concept recurs throughout the book. When she thinks of the properties of Father, Son, and Holy Spirit, she sees him, for example, as Maker, Keeper, Lover, and Might, Wisdom, Goodness (Chapter 5), and All-Might, All-Wisdom, All-Love (Chapter 8), and Life, Love, and Light (Chapter 83). He functions, too, in trinitarian fashion: 'The Father may, the Son can, the Holy Ghost will' do whatever it is he wills (Chapter 31); or 'the Father willeth, our Mother worketh, the Holy Ghost confirmeth' (Chapter 59). The point need not be laboured, for it will strike every reader.

Man, too, is threefold, being 'a made trinity like to the un-made blissful Trinity' (Chapter 55) and is compounded of 'truth, wisdom, and love' (Chapter 44). He possesses 'reason, mind, and love' (Chapter 56) and experiences God through 'nature, mercy, and grace' (Chapter 58). Spiritually, he has need of 'love, longing, and pity' (Chapter 75). One would expect 'faith, hope, and charity' to appear somewhere, and so it does, most fully in Chapter 84. Julian at times seems almost obsessed with numerical analysis: behind it lies her belief in the Triune God.

But above all else God is love, and all his works, natural or spiritual, are done in love. In support of this the last chapter of the *Revelations* is often quoted, and quite rightly so, for it is basic to her whole teaching.

Wouldst thou witten thy Lord's meaning in this thing? Learn it well: love was his meaning. Who shewed it thee? Love. What shewed he thee? Love. Wherefore shewed it he? For love. Hold thee therein, and thou shalt learn and know more in the same. But thou shalt never know nor learn therein other thing without end. Thus was I learned that love was our Lord's meaning. And I saw full surely that ere God made us he loved us; which love was never slacked nor ever shall be. And in this love he hath done all his works; and in this love he hath made all things profitable to us; and in this love our life is everlasting. In our making we had beginning; but the love wherein he made us was in him from without beginning: in which love we have our beginning. And all this shall we see in God, without end.* [Chapter 86]

It is because of this overwhelming certainty of the love of God that Julian's outlook is consistently optimistic and sunny. Not that she is ever starry-eyed. She is puzzled by sin, and darkness and hell, and the Fiend, but she never loses her conviction that love will ultimately triumph, and turn everything to his 'worship'. And because she is on his side – and she is well aware that she is but a symbol of all her 'even-Christians' – she knows that she and all-who-are-to-be-saved will share eternally in the coming Victory. Without trying to see Julian as a child of the Reformation, still less as a revivalist, one can yet believe that she would subscribe to the words of a much-loved mission hymn, 'Blessed assurance, Jesus is mine! O what a foretaste of glory divine!' She is very sure of God.

Everything that exists, everything that happens, whether it

* *Revelations of Divine Love*. Ed. Grace Warrack (Methuen, 1958).

be in the realm of nature or spirit, is upheld by God. Because of this (and no doubt her own experience supported her) she uses epithets of God which are peculiarly her own, and which are found throughout the book. Thus God is 'homely'. For a translator this is a difficult word for which there is no single modern equivalent. It refers to God's intimacy, his familiarity, his domesticity, his interest in every corner of life. 'Closer is he than breathing; nearer than hands and feet.'

God's attitude is always one of 'courtesy'. Without ceasing to control the affairs of the universe, however wayward the human part of it might be, his approach is always that of the perfect gentleman. The wonderful fifty-first chapter, with its long allegory of the lord and his servant, is sufficient illustration of this, but the motif runs through the whole work from Chapters 7 to 85. Perhaps there is a hint here of Julian's background, with God being thought of as a 'verray parfit gentil knight' of girlhood days. Be that as it may, it is a true picture of his dealing with the soul. It is not the complete picture, as Julian herself realizes, for this homely and courteous One is immeasurably great and dreadful, and only to be approached with godly fear (Chapter 73).

For many people the most striking note of Julian's teaching is to be found in Chapters 58 to 63 where her emphasis is on the *motherhood* of God revealed in our Lord. 'Mother' is a word often on her lips. In the earlier, shorter, version she mentions her natural mother (Chapter 10). And there is Holy Mother Church and Mother Mary, Mother of our Lord and of all Christians. But above all else the word means for her our 'Mother Jesus'. 'This fair lovely word *Mother*, it is so sweet . . . that it may not verily be said of none but him.'

This sort of spiritual inversion comes as a shock to most Christians of whatever age, and not least Julian's own. It is true that there can be found some sort of scriptural warrant for regarding God as our Mother (e.g. Isaiah xlix, 1, 15; lxvi,

13; Matt. xxiii, 37), but such as it is, it is far too flimsy for any doctrine to be built upon it. However, some of the medievals developed the idea, and it is thought that Julian was influenced by St Anselm and St Bernard, its chief exponents. It is impossible to say. It is simpler to believe that the teaching is her own, and that blessed with a happy childhood she saw in her own mother's love some reflection of God's care. Either way, she handles the theme with great delicacy and skill. 'We have our being of him, where the ground of motherhood beginneth.' She is thinking of God as Creator of soul and body, and our restorer in mercy. He is therefore 'our Mother in nature and grace'. His work, too, is motherly. The throes of birth are found in the travail of the cross. The milk by which the child of God is suckled is 'the blessed Sacrament that is precious food of my life'. The maternal bosom to which we fly is his wounded side. And just as a human mother changes her tactics, but not her love, as the child grows up, even allowing it to suffer for its own good, so, too, does 'our heavenly Mother, Jesus'. We can run childlike to him for help, and at once 'the sweet gracious hands of our Mother be ready and diligently about us'. Julian believes in God's motherhood because she believes in God's love.

It is improbable that Julian had heard of the primitive Christian doctrine of 'Recapitulation', but it is clear that she has a very thorough grasp of its principles. St Irenaeus (A.D. 130–200), basing himself on hints from St Paul, taught that Christ included within himself all the aspirations and hopes of mankind. The old creation was summed up in Adam; the new creation – and it is new – is summed up in Christ. Everyone and everything is 'recapitulated' in him. What was lost in the old is resumed, re-organized, returned, restored in our Lord. And since Christianity starts with baptism into the Blessed Trinity, the baptized are incorporated into Christ, and share in these blessings. However Julian came by this teaching – and this, too, could be the result of her robust theological thinking, or, even more likely, the effect of the revelations – it underlies all she has to say concerning Christ. All is included in him: he is the true Adam, the essential Mother, the real self, the very heaven. Nothing is lacking in him. Nothing can spoil or mutilate the perfection of all who are in the All.

(*ii*) *Sin*. Julian is not the first to feel the tension rising from the fact of God's love and the existence of sin. She is immensely puzzled, and at times one feels that the independence of her mind is chafing against the leading strings of catholic doctrine. But she is too loyal a daughter of the Church to break through and follow her own uninhibited ideas.

There is the problem of sin itself, best expressed in her own words:

After this the Lord brought to my mind the longing I had to him afore. And I saw that nothing letted me but sin. And so I beheld generally in us all, and methought, 'If sin had not been, we should all have been clean and like to our Lord as he made us.' And thus in my folly afore this time often I wondered why by the great foreseeing wisdom of God the beginning of sin was not letted.*

This is a fair question to ask for one sure of the love of God. The answer given by our Lord is this:

'Sin is behovable' [i.e. necessary or inevitable], 'but all shall be well, and all shall be well, and all manner of thing shall be well.' [Chapter 27]

She accepts this in the immediate context, but it does not satisfy her for she comes back later with this nagging query:

'Ah, good Lord, how might all be well for the great hurt that is come by sin to thy creatures?' (And here I desired, as far as I durst, to have some more open declaring wherewith I might be eased.) [Chapter 29]

* This and the following quotations are taken from B. M., M S. Sloane 2499 (spelling and punctuation modernized).

Our Lord replies that Adam's sin was the most harmful deed ever perpetrated, but the time would come when she would see that the glorious satisfaction of the atonement was incomparably more pleasing to God than ever Adam's sin was hurtful. But she is still puzzled:

One point of our faith is that many creatures shall be damned: as angels that fell out of heaven for pride, which be now fiends; and many on earth that dieth out of the faith of Holy Church, that is to say, they that be heathen men; and also many that hath received Christendom and liveth unchristian life and so dieth out of charity; all these shall be damned to hell without end, as Holy Church teacheth me to believe. And standing all this [i.e., this being so] methought it was impossible that all manner of thing should be well. [Chapter 32]

This time she is told quite simply that what is impossible to man is possible to God, who will keep his word in every respect and 'make all things well'. And there in faith she has to leave it. That strong intellect is trembling on the brink of universalism, but she retains her balance for she will not be 'drawn thereby from any point of the Faith that Holy Church teacheth me to believe' (Chapter 33).

On the whole this determination to be orthodox succeeds in its intention, for her general teaching is in line with that of Holy Church. Thus, sin has no substantive existence however real it may seem to us. In essence it is negative, being what good is not (Chapter 27). All men sin (Chapter 37) and suffer appallingly as a result, feeling themselves deservedly outcast and forsaken (Chapter 39). But God is able to overrule such falling, and to transmute it into something glorious and splendid (Chapter 38). The Fiend has been conquered and spurned (Chapter 13), and his foul brood likewise (Chapter 33). This is all admirably sound and orthodox, but the conflict between God's 'All shall be well' and the fate of the unsaved remains. It has its root in her unwillingness to admit that God can be wrathful. 'In God there may be no wrath,' she declares in Chapter 13 and elsewhere, and by the same token sets aside the teaching of the Bible in both Testaments. The wrath of Yahweh in the Old, and of God incarnate in the New finds no place in her understanding of God's love. This may be very comforting, but it is not the catholic Faith, and it is surprising in one who otherwise is scriptural in her teaching. And because she soft-pedals this difficulty, which with good will and a certain amount of special pleading can be explained away, she lands herself in a much deeper one from which even her friends are unable to extricate her. 'In every soul that shall be saved is a godly will that never assented to sin, nor ever shall' (Chapter 37). Moreover, it always wills what is good, and cannot do otherwise.

This is wishful thinking and not the teaching of the Church. But before one condemns Julian's heterodoxy it must be remembered what it is that she is trying to do. She is attempting to reconcile the fact that good people sin with the promise of eternal life for them in heaven, where there can be no sin. The biblical confidence which accepts the fact of sin, but teaches that, when he forgives, God 'remembers our sins and iniquities no more', 'casting them into the depths of the sea', for 'we are cleansed by Christ's Blood from all sin', is not wholly shared by Julian. She starts from the premise that if a sinner is to be saved there must be in him some part that has *never* sinned, with which God can deal, as it were. As she stands Julian is wrong. One can believe her to have erred from the best of motives. She is striving to preserve in harmony the Allness of God which she has mystically experienced, and the sinlessness of heaven, and the love of God for the sinner, and the refusal of God to impute sin to his elect. She does not quite succeed. Perhaps there is a trace of Meister Eckhardt here, for he believed in an eternal divine spark within every man, which never sinned. Walter Hilton and Ruysbroeck have passages in their works which can be taken in this sense.

Any of these might have influenced Julian, either directly or through the ordinary commerce of current mystical thought. There is no true revelation here, the theologian would say, because it does not accord with accepted dogma. But if a genuine revelation should lie behind it, then the risk of mistranslating so great an experience is a very real one, as this error serves to show.

But there is another possible explanation of Julian's heresy. It has been suggested earlier that her conceptions of the lord and his servant, and of the motherhood of God, might have been influenced by her home background, happy and loving. If this is a legitimate inference, is it pressing too hard to surmise further that, with such an upbringing, Julian might never have seen really malevolent evil in others? She would not be unusual in this respect, and reclusion after her visions would protect rather than instruct her in such sordid matters. And, arguing from the same premise, it is not unreasonable to hold that her views on 'the godly will that never assented to sin' were due to her own personal innocence, and to the probability that in her own life there had never been any deliberate refusal of God. The humility and charity of such a soul would not hesitate to ascribe a like compliance to all her fellow Christians.

(iii) *Prayer.* Although her book deals primarily with sixteen showings of divine love, Julian is at pains to point out that such visions are no indication of sanctity on her part, nor a necessity for another Christian in his spiritual development. She has three chapters on prayer (Chapters 41 to 43), and many references to the subject elsewhere. The specific chapters seem at first sight rather disappointing, until it is remembered that she is writing not for the lowland layman but for those already well up in the contemplative foot-hills. She deals with aridity and faith, and then immediately passes to the thought that all prayer is rooted in God: words, requests, intentions, and all. 'Beseeching' so understood will grow and develop: it is always in harmony with his will, and so is always positively and gladly answered by God. She returns to the subject of 'dry' praying and one of the remedies she suggests is to thank God for his goodness. Her thoughts tumble over each other in glorious confusion. The object of prayer is to be united to our Lord, she declares, and therefore prayers should be bold and broad. Prayer is always answered, even if the response is delayed or altered. Delayed answers help us to see the hand of God in everything, and that includes the prospect of our future joy. Best of all, prayer is the means of union with God. When by the grace and courtesy of our Lord our eyes behold him, then perforce we cease from our intercessions; for 'all our intent with all our might is set wholly to the beholding of him'. Such prayer is indescribable, and complete, delightful and dreadful, sweet and submissive. The whole of Chapter 43 is a fine, warm piece of mystical writing, and it leads the reader right up to the Beatific Vision.

Outside these three chapters there are many references to the subject; too many indeed to be handled in a brief and simple introduction. But three emphases in Julian's orthodoxy are worth noting: (i) She takes for granted the prior disciplines of the 'lower levels of prayer' (Chapters 39 to 40) – and among them is the need for detachment (Chapter 5). For to love God there must be a real freedom from the desire for all good things, though they are still good and splendid things, created by God. Julian is not like some of her colleagues, world-denying. (ii) Prayer is basically a longing for God (Chapter 5 and *passim*). Again and again the English mystics of the fourteenth century remind us that prayer is primarily concerned with God, and not with need. Hence without this intense desire there can be little or no progress in the spiritual life. (iii) Though there are periods of dryness and perplexity, in Julian's teaching there is no sign of any 'dark night' of sense or spirit. This proves nothing, but it serves to underline what seems to be a fact: the dark night, or desert, or dereliction, or what-you-will, depends to a considerable amount on two factors: the temperament of the contemplative, and the nature of his belief. These two factors, of course, interact upon each other. Julian quite clearly was a sanguine and cheerful person, and she had little difficulty in believing in the love and goodness of God. This tremendous grip of faith kept her head well above water, where a less optimistic soul might have been submerged. More than is generally recognized, prior theological suppositions affect subsequent spiritual experience. But they do not govern them, for the effect of the dark night, if outridden, is to produce a personal depth of conviction, and an awareness of God's Being compared with which the earlier 'certainties' are seen to be shallow indeed. Yet Mother Julian shows that not all the routes to the Heavenly City are by underground.

The Outline of the Book

As showings and meditations succeed each other in due order, Julian's thought also moves forward. Its development is not too difficult to follow.

The Love of God Shown in the Cross

She sketches, graphically and skilfully, the context in which the revelations were given (Chapters 2 and 3), and then describes the first group of twelve, which are based on the cross and passion of our Lord (Chapters 4 to 26). The foundation of the Christian Faith is the redemption of mankind effected by Christ's death. This is not only the logical and necessary means of universal salvation, but something which has to be personally appropriated by each individual. So Julian sees first of all the love of God revealed in the death of Christ. The whole Trinity is involved in this love, and each Person plays his part. It is a love that creates and sustains, and which calls for our wholehearted response. But this same loving goodness of God lies behind everything, and the recognition of this fact is the secret of true humility, as the example of our Lady demonstrates. God shows his own humility and courtesy in the cross. The personal faith, trust, and love which this calls forth bring their own particular happiness, coupled with an immense longing to share the knowledge with one's fellows. Yet the experience of God can only be given by God himself. Even though sin may cloud our vision and hinder this experience we still go on seeking him. Further, God is the being of everything that exists, and therefore everything must be good. Sin might seem to be an exception to this, but, of course, it has no substantive being; such stains as it leaves are washed away in the precious blood of Christ. Satan, too, is overcome by the power of the cross. Indeed, the very shame of sin is transmuted by God into a thing of joy. Sin often enough is associated with suffering, and rightly so, but the suffering known by the Christian is not necessarily the result of his wrong-doing: it may well be a test of his fidelity. With sin and suffering still at the back of her mind, Julian returns to the thought of its cure in the crucifixion, and she paints a very vivid and moving picture of our Lord's dying. By its very horror she begins to know what it is to suffer with him – for love always suffers with its beloved – and she sees in the Blessed Virgin the supreme expression of this compassionate love. Julian herself now feels both the revulsion and exaltation of sharing the passion, and in this way comes to realize that the deeper the fellowship of Christ's suffering, the greater is the ultimate joy in heaven. She feels she has now entered his heart of love, and naturally is led on to think of our

Lady, who is the delight of our Lord, and the type of all Christians. But Christ is all, and in all.

Love Triumphs Over Sin

The problem of sin is very real to Julian, and the long thirteenth revelation (Chapters 27 to 40) grapples with the matter. It is the great hindrance to the soul; it is the cause of Christ's passion; yet, as she reminds us again, it has no real existence. Such as it is will be turned into an eternal blessing for the Christian by Christ. 'All will be well' is the repeated assurance. But how? asks Julian. The answer (which may not be thought to be entirely satisfactory by modern minds) is that this is basically God's business and not ours. All *will* be well, for Christ longs for us with a divine thirst not to be gainsaid. Perhaps we may not understand now, but we will on that Day when God chooses to reveal his secrets. His mercy and righteousness are bound to prevail, and we shall rejoice therein. Even if the soul has sinned, there is still within it a godly will that has never consented to it, and because of this God is able to love us, and we are able to please him. God counterbalances every sin of the Christian, and makes it into a much greater blessing than ever it was an evil. He uses it as a scourge as well, to move the soul to contrition and confession and a new start. It even serves to underline God's great love to us.

Love Unites the Soul to God

In the fourteenth revelation she turns to the subject of prayer, the ground of which is our Lord himself (Chapters 41 to 43). Prayer, she says, is always answered, but it must be deliberate, persistent, and grateful. It is most beneficial, and a highly joyful thing moreover, since it unites the soul to God. Her subsequent meditations on this wonderful prospect (Chapters 44 to 63) bring her back to her besetting problem, how to reconcile the judgement of Holy Church on sin, with the love of God who can never be angry. Chapter after chapter is devoted to this subject, while Julian repeatedly asserts the inability of God to be wrathful. The famous fifty-first chapter purports to hold the key, but in fact this splendid allegory of the lord and his servant does not help very much. There is a double significance in this story: the lord stands for God in both instances, in his totality in the first interpretation, and in his Person as Father in the second; the servant is, first, Everyman, and then the Person of the Son. Both interpretations overlap, though the details signify different truths in the two exegeses. It is because of this overlap and subtle connexion that Julian is able to see that the Father, ever loving and never blaming the Son, also loves and does not blame Everyman. Behind this picture lies the persistent refusal to come to terms with the biblical concept of wrath as a part of divine love. The meditations which follow tell of the love of God for his children: he is Father, Brother, Husband to them. Again we are told of the unsinning godly will, which permits God to regard them without blame and to unite himself to them. Indeed, he lives within the soul, and the soul dwells in him; in Christ it is complete; it is all God. This mutual indwelling means that it is in Christ that we come to the Father, in him that we most fully know our own soul, in him that our flesh has been taken into the Godhead. Mary, his mother, is therefore our mother too. But even she is but the shadow of the real Mother, who is Jesus.

Love Brings Us to Heaven

Chapters 64 and 65 give the fifteenth revelation, which is chiefly concerned with the bliss of heaven. We have need of patience while we wait for it. The love of God which heaven displays is such that any suffering we undergo here will be seen to be a mere nothing in comparison with it. It would be more accurate to say that we shall be taken from suffering,

rather than that suffering will be taken from us. The consideration of the bliss of heaven is, for the saved – in other words,
those who love God – both delightful and necessary. Coupled
with this 'blessed assurance' must be a proper fear and a real
humility, for it is these which give us our confidence, and
help us to see suffering in its true perspective.

Now Julian experiences a reaction which is spiritual as well
as physical. With the return of her pain, she denies momen-
tarily the genuineness of the revelations, but at once repents
of such conduct. Falling asleep she has a violent nightmare in
which the Devil is trying to throttle her. This seems to have
been the crisis of her illness, for after it the pain leaves her,
and she is restored in body and spirit. At peace once more, she
receives the sixteenth and final revelation of the soul's dignity
– it is the city where God has his seat, in which he delights to
dwell (Chapters 66 to 70). She is now certain of the soul's
triumph, but (perhaps because of her earlier denial) she is
immediately tested by fresh and continuing temptation to
despair. God's help comes through her belief in the creed of
Holy Church and the passion of our Lord, and she is preserved. There follow in the remaining chapters (71 to 86) a
series of beautiful meditations on various aspects of the revelations. Thus she considers in turn our Lord's regard for us, sin
in the Christian, the fear of God, the loving of God and our
longing for him, his goodness, his honour, and nature. And
the last chapter of all sums it up in words so often quoted,
but capable of standing up to the most frequent repetition -
for is not this a revelation of divine love? – 'Wouldst thou
witten thy Lord's meaning? Learn it well: Love was his meaning.'

Acknowledgements and Further Reading

No one who has written about Julian of Norwich in recent years can be unaware of his indebtedness to Sister Anna Maria Reynolds, s.c. Her knowledge and scholarship have been at the ready disposal of all who have sought it, and the present editor is one of the latest beneficiaries. He wishes to record his deep gratitude for her kindness. Without the help of her learning this introduction would be a very much poorer thing.

But gratitude, too, must be expressed to two others. The Abbot of Nashdom, Dom Augustine Morris, o.s.b., read this translation in typescript and made many helpful suggestions. The difficult task of preparing the typescript itself was done by Muriel Robson, Chapter Clerk of Newcastle Cathedral. Intuition, patience, and a love for Mother Julian enabled her to cope with provostorial illegibility.

There are various editions of the *Revelations of Divine Love*. Three of the most readily procurable, and all bearing the traditional title, have been edited by Grace Warrack (Methuen, 1901; 13th edn 1949), Roger Hudleston (Burns, Oates, 1927; 2nd edn 1952), and James Walsh (Burns, Oates, 1961). In each case the flavour of the Middle English has been preserved, though obsolete words have been modernized. In the latest version, however, the modernization has been much more thorough, with a resultant increase in readability. The shorter version is published as *A Shewing of God's Love*, and is edited by A. M. Reynolds (Longmans, Green & Co., 1958). In every case there is an excellent introduction.

More than most Julian has attracted the attention of writers. One recent book is outstanding for its masterly analysis of her spirituality. It is *Julian of Norwich* by Paul Molinari (Longmans, Green & Co., 1958). It is essential for the student, and one of its many assets is a comprehensive bibliography.

Most books – and they are not a few – which deal with the English Mystics give generous consideration to our solitary, and among the more authoritative are:

Kendall, E. Lorna, *A City not Forsaken*, Faith Press, 1962

Knowles, David, *The English Mystical Tradition*, Burns, Oates, 1961

Pepler, Conrad, *The English Religious Heritage*, Blackfriars, 1958

Renaudin, Paul, *Quatre mystiques anglais*, Éditions du Cerf, 1945

Thornton, Martin, *English Spirituality*, S.P.C.K., 1963

Walsh, James, *Pre-Reformation English Spirituality*, Burns, Oates, 1966

Ancillary books of much interest are:
Anson, Peter, *The Call of the Desert*, S.P.C.K., 1964

Clay, R. M., *The Hermits and Anchorites of England*, Methuen, 1914

Darwin, Francis, D. S., *The English Mediaeval Recluse*, S.P.C.K., no date

Happold, F. C., *Mysticism*, Penguin Books, 1963

Underhill, Evelyn, *Mysticism*, Methuen, 1911

Most of the books on the above list have influenced directly or indirectly this introduction, and the help received therefrom is gratefully acknowledged.

———————

The picture on the cover of this book comes from the great thirteenth century *Amesbury Psalter*, and is reproduced by courtesy of the Warden and Fellows of All Souls College, Oxford, in whose library it is now kept. It represents a nun of the Fontrevault Order praying at the foot of Christ in glory. His attitude to us is one of grace, as the chalice in his hand shows.

Revelations of Divine Love

made to an uneducated person in
A.D. 1373

*A Revelation of Love that Our Lord Jesus Christ,
Our Eternal Bliss, Made in
Sixteen Showings*

LIST OF CHAPTERS

(This analysis of Julian's work was compiled by a later scribe, and is not part of the original book.)

because we know the great love of God we are not to
get careless about falling; if we do not get up at once
after we have fallen we are most unkind to God   202

80. By three things is God worshipped, and we are saved;
our present knowledge is but the ABC; our sweet
Jesus does it all; he abides with us; and grieves for us;
when we sin only he grieves; then it is for us to turn
back to him at once, out of kindness and reverence   204

81. The blessed woman saw God in many ways, but she saw
him take his rest nowhere but in man's soul; his will is
that we rejoice more in his love than we sorrow over
our frequent falls, that we remember the everlasting
reward, and live in glad penitence; why God allows sin   206

82. God looks at the soul's grief with pity, not blame; yet we
do nothing but sin; in it we are kept in solace and fear;
God wants us to turn to him, and cling to his love,
and see him to be our medicine; we must love, in
longing and enjoyment; anything opposed to this
comes from the enemy, not God   207

83. Three attributes of God: life, love, and light; our reason
agrees; it is God's greatest gift; our faith is a light
which comes from the Father; it is measured to our
need, and leads us through the night; at the end of our
troubles our eyes will be opened suddenly; this full
light and clarity is God our Maker, Father, and Holy
Spirit, through Jesus, our Saviour   208

84. This light is charity; it is not so insignificant as not to be
needed; we are to strive to deserve the eternal and
glorious gratitude of God; faith and hope lead us to
charity, and its three modes   209

85. God loved his elect from all time; he never allows them
to be hurt so that their bliss is lessened; secrets now

1 THE Revelations in detail: The first revelation tells of Christ's precious crowning with thorns. It included and demonstrated the Trinity, the incarnation, and the unity between God and the soul of man. There were many splendid revelations of eternal wisdom, and many lovely lessons about love, and all the subsequent revelations are based on these. (*Chapters 4–9, page 66*)

The second concerns the discolouring of his fair face, the sign of his most dear passion. (*Chapter 10, page 76*)

The third shows that our Lord God, almighty, all-wisdom, and all-love, has made everything, and also works in and through everything. (*Chapter 11, page 80*)

The fourth speaks of the flogging of that tender body, and of the blood shed copiously. (*Chapter 12, page 82*)

The fifth reveals that the Fiend is conquered through Christ's pitiful passion. (*Chapter 13, page 83*)

The sixth describes the great honour of God's gratitude and the heavenly reward for his blessed servants. (*Chapter 14, page 85*)

The seventh depicts the recurring experience of delight and depression. The former is God's touch of grace and radiance, and brings real assurance of eternal joy; the latter is a temptation caused by the dullness and frustration of our life in the body. There is the spiritual knowledge that we are kept secure in love, through delight and depression, by God's goodness. (*Chapter 15, page 86*)

The eighth speaks of Christ's final sufferings and his cruel death. (*Chapters 16–21, page 87*)

The ninth relates the pleasure that the Blessed Trinity has in the grievous passion of Christ, and his pitiful death. In this joy and pleasure God wants us to be comforted and cheered along with him until we come to our fulfilment in heaven. (*Chapters 22–23, page 96*)

The tenth shows our Lord Jesus rejoicing to display, in his love, his blessed heart, riven in two. (*Chapter 24, page 100*)

The eleventh is a high and spiritual revelation of his beloved Mother. (*Chapter 25, page 101*)

The twelfth shows our Lord to be the being of all that is, and most worthy. (*Chapter 26, page 102*)

The thirteenth declares the will of God to be that we should greatly value all his works: the noble nature of all creation, the excellency of man's creation, the supremest of his works, and the precious atonement he has made for man's sin, turning our blame into eternal splendour. He says, 'Look. By my same mighty wisdom and goodness I shall make what is not right to be all right. And you shall see it.' In all this it is his will that we hold on to the Faith and truth of Holy Church, and be not anxious to know his secrets now, but only in so far as we are able in this life. (*Chapters 27–40, page 103*)

The fourteenth reveals that our Lord is the foundation of our prayers. There are two considerations here: right praying, and sure trust. He wants both alike to be generous. So our prayer will delight him, and through his goodness he will answer it. (*Chapters 41–63, page 123*)

The fifteenth says that we shall be taken suddenly from all our pain and distress and by the goodness of God attain heaven, where the Lord Jesus will be our reward, and we shall be filled with joy and bliss. (*Chapters 64–65, page 177*)

The sixteenth affirms that the Blessed Trinity, our Creator in Christ Jesus our Saviour, lives eternally in our soul. There he rules in honour and governs all things; by his might and wisdom he saves and keeps us for love's sake; we will not be overcome by our enemy. (*Chapters 66–86, page 181*)

The time of the revelations, and Julian's three petitions

2 THESE revelations were shown to a simple and un-educated creature on the eighth of May 1373. Some time earlier she had asked three gifts from God: (i) to understand his passion; (ii) to suffer physically while still a young woman of thirty; and (iii) to have as God's gift three wounds.

With regard to the first I thought I had already had some experience of the passion of Christ, but by his grace I wanted still more. I wanted to be actually there with Mary Magdalene and the others who loved him, and with my own eyes to see and know more of the physical suffering of our Saviour, and the compassion of our Lady and of those who there and then were loving him truly and watching his pains. I would be one of them and suffer with him. I had no desire for any other vision of God until after such time as I had died. The reason for this prayer was that I might more truly understand the passion of Christ.

The second came to me with much greater urgency. I quite sincerely wanted to be ill to the point of dying, so that I might receive the last rites of Holy Church, in the belief – shared by my friends – that I was in fact dying. There was no earthly comfort I wanted to live for. In this illness I wanted to undergo all those spiritual and physical sufferings I should have were I really dying, and to know, moreover, the terror and assaults of the demons – everything, except death itself! My intention was that I should be wholly cleansed thereby through the mercy of God, and that thereafter, because of that illness, I might live more worthily of him. Perhaps too I might even die a better death, for I was longing to be with my God.

There was a condition with these two desires: 'Lord, you know what I am wanting. If it is your will that I have it. . . . But if not, do not be cross, good Lord, for I want nothing but your will.'

As for the third, through the grace of God and the teaching of Holy Church I developed a strong desire to receive three wounds, namely, the wound of true contrition, the wound of genuine compassion, and the wound of sincere longing for God. There was no proviso attached to any part of this third prayer.

I forgot all about the first two desires, but the third was with me continually.

The illness thus obtained from God

3 WHEN I was half way through my thirty-first year God sent me an illness which prostrated me for three days and nights. On the fourth night I received the last rites of Holy Church as it was thought I could not survive till day. After this I lingered two more days and nights, and on the third night I was quite convinced that I was passing away – as indeed were those about me.

Since I was still young I thought it a great pity to die – not that there was anything on earth I wanted to live for, or on the other hand any pain that I was afraid of, for I trusted God and his mercy. But were I to live I might come to love God more and better, and so ultimately to know and love him more in the bliss of heaven. Yet compared with that eternal bliss the length of my earthly life was so insignificant and short that it seemed to me to be nothing. And so I thought, 'Good Lord, let my ceasing to live be to your glory!' Reason and suffering alike told me I was going to die, so I surrendered my will wholeheartedly to the will of God.

Thus I endured till day. By then my body was dead from the waist downwards, so far as I could tell. I asked if I might be helped and supported to sit up, so that my heart could be more freely at God's disposal, and that I might think of him while my life lasted.

My parish priest was sent for to be at my end, and by the time he came my eyes were fixed, and I could no longer speak. He set the cross before my face and said, 'I have brought you the image of your Maker and Saviour. Look at it, and be strengthened.'

I thought indeed that what I was doing was good enough, for my eyes were fixed heavenwards where by the mercy of God I trusted to go. But I agreed none the less to fix my eyes on the face of the crucifix if I could. And this I was able to do. I thought that perhaps I could look straight ahead longer than I could look up.

Then my sight began to fail, and the room became dark about me, as if it were night, except for the image of the cross which somehow was lighted up; but how was beyond my comprehension. Apart from the cross everything else seemed horrible as if it were occupied by fiends.

Then the rest of my body began to die, and I could hardly feel a thing. As my breathing became shorter and shorter I knew for certain that I was passing away.

Suddenly all my pain was taken away, and I was as fit and well as I had ever been; and this was especially true of the lower part of my body. I was amazed at this sudden change, for I thought it must have been a special miracle of God, and not something natural. And though I felt so much more comfortable I still did not think I was going to survive. Not that this experience was any real comfort to me, for I was thinking I would much rather have been delivered from this world!

Then it came suddenly to mind that I should ask for the second wound of our Lord's gracious gift, that I might in my own body fully experience and understand his blessed passion. I wanted his pain to be my pain: a true compassion producing a longing for God. I was not wanting a physical vision or revelation of God, but such compassion as a soul would naturally have for our Lord Jesus, who for love became a mortal man. Therefore I desired to suffer with him.

The first revelation: the precious crowning of Christ; God fills the heart with the greatest joy; Christ's great humility; the sight of his passion is sufficient strength against all the temptations of the fiends; the glory and humility of the Blessed Virgin Mary

4 AND at once I saw the red blood trickling down from under the garland,* hot, fresh, and plentiful, just as it did at the time of his passion when the crown of thorns was pressed on to the blessed head of God-and-Man, who suffered for me. And I had a strong, deep, conviction that it was he himself and none other that showed me this vision.

At the same moment the Trinity filled me full of heartfelt joy, and I knew that all eternity was like this for those who attain heaven. For the Trinity is God, and God the Trinity; the Trinity is our Maker and keeper, our eternal lover, joy and bliss – all through our Lord Jesus Christ. This was shown me in this first revelation, and, indeed, in them all; for where Jesus is spoken of, the blessed Trinity is always to be understood as I see it.

* i.e. the crown of thorns.

'*Benedicite Domine!*'* I said, and I meant it in all reverence even though I said it at the top of my voice. I was overwhelmed with wonder that he, so holy and aweful, could be so friendly to a creature at once sinful and carnal. I took it that all this was to prepare me for a time of temptation, for I thought that by God's leave I was bound to be tempted by fiends before I died. With this sight of the blessed passion, and with my mental vision of the Godhead, I knew that there was strength enough for me and, indeed, for every living creature against every fiend of hell, and all temptation.

And then he brought our blessed Lady to mind. In my spirit I saw her as though she were physically present, a simple humble girl, still in her youth, and little more than a child. God showed me something of her spiritual wisdom and honesty, and I understood her profound reverence when she saw her God and Maker; how reverently she marvelled that he should be born of his own creature, and of one so simple. This wisdom and honesty, which recognized the greatness of her Creator and the smallness of her created self, moved her to say to Gabriel in her utter humility, 'Behold the handmaid of the Lord!' By this I knew for certain that in worth and grace she is above all that God made, save the blessed humanity of Christ.

God is all that is good, and gently enfolds us; in comparison with almighty God creation is nothing; man can have no rest until he totally denies himself and everything else for love of God

5 IT was at this time that our Lord showed me spiritually how intimately he loves us. I saw that he is everything that we know to be good and helpful. In his love he clothes us,

* Literally: 'Bless ye, O Lord' – '*Benedicite*' is the traditional greeting of religious to each other; almost, 'Welcome!'.

enfolds and embraces us; that tender love completely surrounds us, never to leave us. As I saw it he is everything that is good.

And he showed me more, a little thing, the size of a hazel-nut, on the palm of my hand, round like a ball. I looked at it thoughtfully and wondered, 'What is this?' And the answer came, 'It is all that is made.' I marvelled that it continued to exist and did not suddenly disintegrate; it was so small. And again my mind supplied the answer, 'It exists, both now and for ever, because God loves it.' In short, everything owes its existence to the love of God.

In this 'little thing' I saw three truths. The first is that God made it; the second is that God loves it; and the third is that God sustains it. But what he is who is in truth Maker, Keeper, and Lover I cannot tell, for until I am essentially united with him I can never have full rest or real happiness; in other words, until I am so joined to him that there is absolutely nothing between my God and me. We have got to realize the littleness of creation and to see it for the nothing that it is before we can love and possess God who is uncreated. This is the reason why we have no ease of heart or soul, for we are seeking our rest in trivial things which cannot satisfy, and not seeking to know God, almighty, all-wise, all-good. He is true rest. It is his will that we should know him, and his pleasure that we should rest in him. Nothing less will satisfy us. No soul can rest until it is detached from all creation. When it is deliberately so detached for love of him who is all, then only can it experience spiritual rest.

God showed me too the pleasure it gives him when a simple soul comes to him, openly, sincerely and genuinely. It seems to me as I ponder this revelation that when the Holy Spirit touches the soul it longs for God rather like this; 'God, of your goodness give me yourself, for you are sufficient for me. I cannot properly ask anything less, to be worthy of you. If I were to ask less, I should always be in want. In you alone do I have all.'

Such words are dear indeed to the soul, and very close to the will and goodness of God. For his goodness enfolds every one of his creatures and all his blessed works, eternally and surpassingly. For he himself is eternity, and has made us for himself alone, has restored us by his blessed passion, and keeps us in his blessed love. And all because he is goodness.

How we should pray; our Lord's great and tender love for the soul of man; his will is that we should busy ourselves in loving and knowing him

6 THE purpose of this revelation was to teach our soul the wisdom of cleaving to the goodness of God. And so our customary practice of prayer was brought to mind: how through our ignorance and inexperience in the ways of love we spend so much time on petition. I saw that it is indeed more worthy of God and more truly pleasing to him that through his goodness we should pray with full confidence, and by his grace cling to him with real understanding and unshakeable love, than that we should go on making as many petitions as our souls are capable of. For however numerous our petitions they still come short of being wholly worthy of him. For in his goodness is included all one can want, without exception.

As I am saying, at this time my mind was reflecting thus: we are able to pray to God because of his holy incarnation, his precious blood, his holy passion, his most dear death and wounds. The blessed consequence of all this, eternal life, springs from his goodness. When we pray for love of the sweet Mother who bore him, the help she gives is due to his goodness. And if we pray by the holy cross on which he died, the strength and the help we get through that cross is through his goodness. Similarly the help that comes from particular saints and the blessed company of heaven, the delightful love and eternal fellowship we enjoy with them, are all due to his goodness. For through his goodness God has ordained the means to help us, both glorious and many. The chief of these is the blessed nature he took of the Maid Mary with all the resultant means of grace which concern our redemption and everlasting salvation. Therefore he is pleased that we should see him and worship him by these means, knowing and realizing that he is the goodness of it all.

To know the goodness of God is the highest prayer of all, and it is a prayer that accommodates itself to our most lowly needs. It quickens our soul, and vitalizes it, developing it in grace and virtue. Here is the grace most appropriate to our need, and most ready to help. Here is the grace which our soul is seeking now, and which it will ever seek until that day when we know for a fact that he has wholly united us to himself. He does not despise the work of his hands, nor does he disdain to serve us, however lowly our natural need may be. He loves the soul he has made in his own likeness.

For just as the body is clothed in its garments, and the flesh in its skin, and the bones in their flesh, and the heart in its body, so too are we, soul and body, clothed from head to foot in the goodness of God. Yes, and even more closely than that, for all these things will decay and wear out, whereas the goodness of God is unchanging, and incomparably more suited to us. Our lover desires indeed that our soul should cleave to him with all its might, and ever hold on to his goodness. Beyond our power to imagine does this most please God, and speed the soul on its course.

The love of God Most High for our soul is so wonderful that it surpasses all knowledge. No created being can know the greatness, the sweetness, the tenderness of the love that our Maker has for us. By his grace and help therefore let us in spirit stand and gaze, eternally marvelling at the supreme, surpassing, singleminded, incalculable love that God, who is goodness, has for us. Then we can ask reverently of our lover whatever we will. For by nature our will wants God, and the good will of God wants us. We shall never cease wanting and longing until we possess him in fulness and joy. Then we shall have no further wants. Meanwhile his will is that we go on knowing and loving until we are perfected in heaven.

It was for this reason that this lesson of love was shown, with all that follows from it, as you will see. For the strength and foundation of it all was revealed in the first vision. More than anything else, it is the loving contemplation of its Maker that causes the soul to realize its own insignificance, and fills it with holy fear and true humility, and with abundant love to our fellow Christians.

Our Lady sees the Creator's greatness, and her own insignificance; the great drops of blood running down from the crown of thorns; man's greatest joy is to know almighty God's holiness and courtesy

7 So at the same time our Lord God, in order to teach this lesson, showed me our Lady, St Mary, and the true and outstanding wisdom which made her gaze on her Maker, so great, high, mighty, and good. The greatness and splendour of her vision of God filled her with holy dread, and caused her to see herself for the insignificant, lowly, simple creature she was compared with her Lord God. And holy dread filled her with humility. Because of this basic humility she was filled with grace and every virtue, thereby surpassing all creation.

All the time he was showing these things to my inward sight, I still seemed to see with my actual eyes the continual bleeding of his head. Great drops of blood rolled down from the garland like beads, seemingly from the veins; and they came down a brownish red colour – for the blood was thick – and as they spread out they became bright red, and when they reached his eyebrows they vanished. Nonetheless the bleeding continued for all the time that there were things for me to see and understand. They were as fresh and living as though they were real: their abundance like the drops of water that fall from the eaves after a heavy shower, falling so thickly that no one can possibly count them; their roundness as they spread out on his forehead were like the scales of herring. I was reminded of these three things at the time: round beads as the blood flowed, round herring scales as it spread out, and raindrops from the eaves for their abundance.

This revelation was real and lifelike, horrifying and dreadful, sweet and lovely. The greatest comfort I received from it was to know that our God and Lord, so holy and aweful, is so unpretentious and considerate. This filled me with comfort and assurance. And so that I could understand it he gave me a clear illustration.

The greatest honour a great king or noble lord can do a poor servant is to treat him as a friend, especially if, in public and private alike, it is seen to be both genuine and spontaneous. The poor man will think something like this, 'What greater honour or pleasure could my noble lord confer on me than to show a simple man like me such marvellous friendliness? Indeed, it gives me much more pleasure than would the greatest gifts if they were bestowed condescendingly.' This physical illustration was showed so vividly that it demonstrated the man's heartfelt delight and almost delirious joy at such great friendliness.

It is the same with our Lord Jesus and ourselves. Surely there can be no greater joy – at least as I see it – than that he, the most supreme, mighty, noble, and worthy of all, should also be the most lowly, humble, friendly, and considerate. In very truth this marvellous joy will be ours when we see him. His will for us is that we should seek for and trust him, rejoice and delight in him, while he in turn strengthens and comforts us until such time as we realize it all in very fact. As I see it, the fullest joy we can have springs from the marvellous consideration and friendliness shown us by our Father and our Maker, through our Lord Jesus Christ, our Brother and our Saviour.

But this wonderful friendliness no living man can know unless it is specially shown him by our Lord, or given him by the inward, abundant grace of the Holy Spirit. Yet faith and trust and love earn their own reward; and, indeed, the reward is had this way, by grace. For it is on faith, hope, and love that our life is based. The revelation, shown to whomsoever God chooses, clearly teaches this, plainly for all to see – and many other hidden things of faith too, of great worth. And when the vision which was given at some particular time has passed and gone, then faith retains it by the grace of the Holy Spirit till the end of our life. The revelation shows that it all depends on faith, no more and no less; for as we can see from our Lord's teaching on the same matter, it is faith that counts at the last.

The previous matter restated; what is shown to Julian in particular is meant for all in general

8 ALL the while I saw the head bleeding so freely I kept ceaselessly saying, '*Benedicite Domine!*'

In this revelation I saw six things: (i) the tokens of his blessed passion, and the copious shedding of his precious blood, (ii) the maid who is his beloved Mother, (iii) the blessed God who always has been, is now, and ever shall be: almighty, all-wise, all-loving, (iv) the whole creation – I was well aware that the universe is great and huge, beautiful and good, but the reason why it seemed so small was that I saw it in the presence of him who is its Creator: and to a soul who sees the Creator of all everything seems insignificant, (v) God who made everything because of his love, by the same love sustains it in being, now and for ever, (vi) God is all that is good, as I see it, and himself is the goodness of all good things.

All this our Lord showed me in this first vision, amply and unhurriedly. When actual sight ceased, my inward sight persisted, and I remained in holy awe, rejoicing at what I saw. And I dared to want to see more, should he will it, or else to retain the present vision longer.

Throughout all this I was greatly moved with love for my fellow Christians, that they might know and see what I was seeing, for I wanted it to cheer them too. The vision was for all and sundry. Then I said to those around me, 'Today is the Day of Judgement for me.' I said this because I thought I was dying. As I understand it, on the day he dies a man is judged eternally. I said this because I wanted them to love God, and to remind them who had an example in me, that life is short. I was sure I was dying, and this to me was a cause both of wonder and disquiet, for I thought the vision was meant for those who were going on living. And though I speak of myself I am really speaking of all my fellow Christians, for I was taught by the inner meaning of this revelation that God intends this. So I beg you all for God's sake, and advise you for your own, to stop thinking about the poor wretch who was shown these things, and with all your strength, wisdom, and humility look at God, that in his loving courtesy and eternal goodness he may be willing to show it to all and sundry, to our own great comfort. For it is God's will that you should receive it with great joy and pleasure, as if Jesus himself had showed it to you all.

Julian's humility keeps her always in the Faith of Holy Church;
*   he who loves his fellow Christian for God's sake loves every-*
*   thing*

9 THE fact that I have had this revelation does not mean that
I am good. I am good only in so far as I love God the
better: if you love God more than do I then you are by that
much better than I. I am not trying to tell the wise something
they know well already; but I am seeking to tell the un-
instructed, for their great peace and comfort. And of comfort
we all have need. It was certainly not shown me because God
loved me more than other lowly souls in grace, for I am quite
sure there must be many who have never had any sort of
revelation or vision beyond the ordinary teaching of Holy
Church, and who yet love God better than I. When I look at
myself in particular I am obviously of no account, but by and
large I am hopeful, for I am united in love with all my fellow
Christians.

It is upon this unity that all those of mankind who are to be
saved must depend. God, as I see it, is everything that is good;
he has made the whole of creation, and loves all that he has
made. And whoever loves his fellow Christians for God, loves
all there is. For everything is included in the 'mankind who
are to be saved': everything, I say, that has been created, and
the Maker of all as well! For God is in man, and God is in
everything. And by the grace of God I hope that anyone who
looks at it in this way will be taught aright, and greatly comforted if need be.

I am speaking only of those who are to be saved, for in this
matter God did not show me otherwise. I shall always believe
what is held, preached, and taught by Holy Church. For the
Faith of Holy Church which I had understood from the first,
and which I hope by the grace of God I had consciously kept

and lived by, was ever before my eyes. I was determined never to accept anything that was contrary to this, so it was with this well in mind that I looked at the revelation so diligently. And in this blessed revelation I saw nothing counter to what had been already revealed.

All this was shown me in three ways, in actual vision, in imaginative understanding, and in spiritual sight. This last I cannot, and may not, disclose as openly and fully as I should like. But I trust that God almighty will of his goodness and love enable you to savour its spirit and sweetness more than my feeble efforts permit.

The second revelation: the change of colour in Christ's face; our redemption; the discolouring of the handkerchief; God is pleased when we seek him diligently, wait on him steadfastly, and trust him wholeheartedly

10 AFTER this I saw with my own eyes in the face of the crucifix hanging before me and at which I was ceaselessly gazing something of his passion. I saw insults and spittle and disfiguring and bruising, and lingering pain more than I know how to describe: and there were frequent changes of colour. On one occasion I saw that half his face, from side to centre, was covered with dry blood, and that afterwards the other half similarly was covered, the first half clearing as the second came.

All this I saw physically, yet obscurely and mysteriously. But I wanted to see it even more vividly and clearly. To my mind came the answer, 'If God wills to show you more, he will be your light. You need none but him.' It was he whom I saw and yet sought. For here we are so blind and foolish that we never seek God until he, of his goodness, shows himself to us. It is when we do see something of him by his grace that we are stirred by that same grace to seek him, and with earnest longing to see still more of his blessedness.

So I saw him and sought him; I had him and wanted him. It seems to me that this is and should be an experience common to us all.

On another occasion I was led in imagination down on to the sea-bed, and there I saw green hills and valleys looking as though they were moss-covered, with seaweed and sand. This I understood to mean that if a man or woman were under-sea and saw God ever present with him (as indeed God is) he would be safe in body and soul, and take no hurt. Moreover he would know comfort and consolation beyond all power to tell. For God's will is that by faith we should see him continually, though it seems to us that we are seeing him so little. By this faith he makes us ever to gain grace. His will is to be seen; his will is to be sought; his will is to be awaited and trusted.

This second revelation seemed so ordinary and commonplace that I was much perplexed when I saw it. I was worried, afraid, and anxious, wondering for some time whether it were in fact a revelation. Then it was that at different times our good Lord gave me greater insight, so that I knew indeed that this was a revelation. It was a picture and a likeness of the shame that our foul deeds caused, and which our fair, splendid, and blessed Lord bore for our sins. It made me think of the Holy Handkerchief* at Rome on which he imprinted his own blessed features at the time of his cruel passion, for when he was going willingly to his death he suffered much change of colour. Many people are surprised that this likeness should be brown and black, downcast and wan, since he who imprinted

---

* The cloth with which, tradition says, St Veronica wiped the face of our Lord on his way to Calvary, and which thereafter bore the imprint of his face. It is preserved in St Peter's, Rome.

on it his blessed face is the fairest of heaven, the flower of the earth, and the fruit of the maiden's womb. How then should this likeness be so pale and so unbeautiful? Let me say how I, by the grace of God, understand it.

We know from our creed, and believe through the teaching and preaching of Holy Church, that the blessed Trinity makes mankind in his image and likeness. In the same way we know that when man fell so deeply and wretchedly through sin there was no other help forthcoming to restore him but from him who made man. And he who out of love made man, by the same love would restore him not merely to his former bliss but to one that was even greater. Just as we were made like the Trinity at our first creation, so our Maker would have us like our Saviour Jesus Christ, in heaven for ever by virtue of our re-creation.

Between these two creations he willed – out of love for man – to make himself as like man, in all our wretchedness and filth, as is possible without sin. Which means, as I have already said, that it was the image and likeness of our foul, black, shameful deeds that hid the fair, splendid, and blessed Lord God. We can say, I think, and believe with every confidence, that never was there a man as fair as he until that time that his beauty was marred by his suffering, his sorrows, his passion, and his death. This is dealt with more fully in the eighth revelation, which has to do with the same subject. And where it speaks of the Handkerchief at Rome, it refers to the different changes of colour and expression, which sometimes are more reassuring and living, sometimes more downcast and death-like, as can be seen from the eighth revelation.

This vision taught me that the continual seeking of the soul for God is greatly pleasing to him, for all it can do is to seek, endure and trust. And this the soul achieves by the Holy Spirit; and the certainty that it has found God comes through his special grace, when he so wills. The seeking, with faith, hope, and charity, pleases our Lord, and the finding pleases and rejoices the soul. In this way I was taught that seeking is as good as seeing all the while God allows the soul to suffer. God's will is that we should seek him in order that we might see him. What is more, it is when he wills that he shows himself, and then by special grace. How to maintain this vision God himself will teach the soul – which, of course, befits him and benefits us, for then it is that through the grace and guidance of the Holy Spirit the soul best comes by humility and virtue. For when a soul cleaves solely to God with a genuine trust, seeking or seeing him, I think it is doing the most honour to him that it can.

The work that this vision depicts is twofold: seeking and seeing. There is nothing very special about seeking. It is a thing that every soul can do with God's grace, and do with the common sense and teaching of Holy Church. God's will is that we should do three things in our seeking: (i) that by his grace we should seek with deliberation and diligence without slacking, and do it moreover gladly and cheerfully without moroseness or melancholy, (ii) that we wait steadfastly on him in love, and do not grumble or gird against him in this life – which is not very long anyway – and (iii) that we trust him wholeheartedly and confidently. This is his will.

We know that he will appear unexpectedly and with great joy to all who love him. He works in secret, yet he wills to be seen. His appearing will be delightful and unexpected. His will is that we trust him, him who is utterly kind and unassuming. Blessings on him!

The third revelation: God does everything except sin; his purpose never varies; he has made everything perfect and good

11 AFTER this I saw the whole Godhead concentrated as it were in a single point,* and thereby I learnt that he is in all things. I looked attentively, seeing and understanding with quiet fear. I was thinking 'What is sin?'

For I saw that God in fact does everything, however little that thing may be. Indeed, nothing happens by luck or chance, but all is through the foresight and wisdom of God. If it seems chance or luck to us, it is because we are blind and short-sighted. Things which God's wise foreknowledge saw before creation, and which he so rightly and worthily and constantly brings to their proper end in due time, break upon us suddenly and take us by surprise. And because of this blindness and lack of foresight we say they are chances and hazards. But they are not so to our Lord God.

Hence it follows that we must admit that everything that is done is well done, for it is our Lord God who does it. How God functions in his creatures was showed me at this time; not how they function in themselves. God is the focal point of everything, and he does it all. And I was sure he does no sin!

From this I gathered that sin is not a thing that we do, not a deed, for in all that was *done*, there was no sin shown. No longer need I wonder at this, but now would look to our Lord, awaiting his revealing. To this extent

---

* This surprising but not uncommon mystical symbol stands for many things; for example: God's centrality – he is the mid-point of the circle of being, and everything is dependent upon him; God's immateriality – a point cannot have material substance; God's immeasurability – one cannot measure it; God's unity – a point is one.

then, the righteousness of God's actions was shown to my soul.

There are two good things about righteousness. It is right and it is perfect, like all the works of our Lord God. It has need neither of mercy nor of grace, for they too are righteous. Nothing is lacking.

There was another time when God gave a revelation; I saw sin in all its nakedness, as I shall tell later; in which his mercy and grace are involved.

This vision helped me to understand that our Lord wants the soul really to be turned to him so that it can gaze on him, and on all his works generally. For they are wholly good. All that he does is comforting and delightful, and brings great comfort to that soul which turns away from considering blindly things that are merely human to consider rather the delightfulness of God. A man will reckon some things to be well done, and others to be evil, but our Lord does not see them so. For as all natural things have been made by God, so all that has been done is in some ways God's doing. It is not difficult to see that the best deed has been done well, and as the best and highest deed has been done, so the least deed has been done just as well. All this is in accordance with the nature and plan that God has decided for everything from before creation. There is no doer but he.

I saw with absolute certainty that he never changes his purpose in anything whatever, and never will. Through his ordering everything has been known to him from the first. It was all set in order before a thing was made, and so it was ever to remain. Nothing shall fail of his purpose. He made all things in abundant goodness, and therefore the Trinity is for ever satisfied with what he has done.

He showed me all this to my great happiness, as if he were saying, 'Look, I am God. I am in all. I do everything! I never cease upholding my work, and I never will. I am guiding everything toward the end I ordained for it from the first, by the same might, wisdom, and love with which I made it. How can anything be wrong?'

In such a way was my soul instructed by this vision, powerfully, wisely, and lovingly. And I saw in truth that I could not do other than assent to it; and so I did, with great reverence and joy in God.

The fourth revelation: God prefers that we should be washed from our sin in his own blood rather than in water; his blood is most precious

12 AFTER this I looked, and saw the body which was bleeding copiously, apparently as the result of the flogging. The fair skin was broken and there were deep weals in the tender flesh of that dear, smitten body. So copious was the hot flow that neither skin nor wound could be seen: it was all blood. Yet when one might have expected it to have poured to the ground it vanished. Yet the bleeding continued and could be seen by attentive eyes. To me it seemed so copious that had it been real the whole bed and more would have been soaked with blood.

And I recalled the truth that though God through his compassionate love has made an abundant supply of water on earth for our use and comfort, he wishes us to use quite simply his blessed blood to wash ourselves clean of sin. For there is no comparable fluid that he would so like to give us. Of all it is at once the most copious and most costly (because it is divine), and, because of his great love, it is the most suitable and gladdening we could want.

The most precious blood of our Lord Jesus Christ is in truth both costly and copious. Look and see. The costly and copious flood of his most precious blood streamed down into hell, and burst the chains, and freed all there who belonged to the Court of Heaven. The costly and copious flood of his most precious blood overflows the whole of earth, and is available to wash all creatures (if they are willing) from their sin, present, past, or future. The costly and copious flood of his most precious blood ascends up to heaven, to our Lord's blessed body itself, and is found there in him, who bleeds and pleads for us with the Father – and that for as long as need shall require. For ever it flows through all heaven, rejoicing to save mankind, such as are there already and those who are yet to come, making up the number of the saints.

The fifth revelation: temptation by the Fiend is overcome by the passion of Christ, which increases our joy and the devil's discomfort everlastingly

13 Then, before he spoke to me, God allowed me to look at himself for a considerable time, and, as far as my simple mind could take it, to dwell on all that I had seen, and its significance. And, without voice or speech, he framed in my soul these words: 'By this is the Fiend overcome.' These words were said by our Lord, and referred to his passion which he had shown me earlier.

By this our Lord revealed that it is his passion that overcomes the Fiend, and that the Fiend is as evilly disposed now as he was before the incarnation. However hard he works, just as often he sees all souls escape him, saved by the worth and virtue of Christ's precious passion. This is grief and shame to him, for whatever God allows him to do turns to our joy and to his shame and woe. It is just as much a cause of grief when God gives him leave to work as when he is not working, because he can never do all the evil that he wants. His power is in God's control.

As I see it there is no anger in God, for our blessed Lord has eternal regard to the honour which is his due and to the benefit of all those who are to be saved. To the malice and cunning with which the reprobate work against the will of God he opposed his might and right. I saw our Lord scorn such malice, and expose the emptiness of the Fiend's powerlessness; and it is his will that we should do the same. When I saw this I laughed so heartily that it made those around me laugh too, and their laughter did me good. I thought I would have liked all my fellow Christians to have seen what I saw, that they might laugh with me. But I did not see Christ laugh. I understood that we may laugh when we would comfort ourselves and rejoice in God that the devil has been overcome. When I saw him scorn his malice, it was by intuition: it was an inner perception of reality; his countenance was unchanged. For to my mind it is a most worthy characteristic of God that he is always the same.

After all this I became more serious. 'I can see three things,' I said. 'A game, a scorning, and an earnestness. A game, in which the Fiend has been overcome: a scorning, because God scorns him, so he shall be scorned indeed; and an earnestness, because he has been overpowered by the blessed passion and death of our Lord Jesus Christ, which was done in real earnest and with real hard work.'

When I say 'he is scorned' I mean that God scorns him, for he sees him now as he ever will be. Thus God shows that the Fiend is damned. This was my meaning when I said 'he shall be scorned'. I was thinking of the Day of Judgement, and the scorn with which the saved will regard him – whose bliss he greatly covets. At that day he will see that all the hurt and hardship he has inflicted upon them has turned to their increasing and eternal joy – and all the pain and hardship he brought them will be eternally his in hell!

The sixth revelation: the great honour of Christ's gratitude with which he rewards his servants; its three joys

14 AFTER this the Lord said, 'Thank you for all your suffering, the suffering of your youth.'

I saw in my imagination heaven, and our Lord as the head of his own house, who had invited all his dear servants and friends to a great feast. The Lord, I saw, occupied no one place in particular in his house, but presided regally over it all, suffusing it with joy and cheer. Utterly at home, and with perfect courtesy, himself was the eternal happiness and comfort of his beloved friends, the marvellous music of his unending love showing in the beauty of his blessed face. Which glorious countenance of the Godhead fills heaven full of joy and delight.

God showed me the three degrees of bliss enjoyed by every soul who has served him deliberately in any way on earth: (i) The most valuable thanks that God shall give him when he is relieved of his suffering. This gratitude is so supremely worthwhile that a man would think he was filled with it even if there were no more. I thought that *all* the pain and suffering experienced by mankind would not merit the worth of the gratitude that a single soul shall get for having deliberately served God! (ii) All blessed heavenly beings are aware of that most worthwhile gratitude, for God makes a man's service known to all heaven. An example of this was given: If a king thanks his servants, they value it greatly, but if he makes it known throughout his realm, then is its value greatly increased. (iii) The freshness and pleasure with which it is at first received shall last for ever.

This also was disclosed to me, with delightful simplicity, that every man's age is to be made known in heaven, and his reward is governed by the willingness of his service and its duration. In particular those who willingly and freely offer their youth to God are rewarded and thanked, supremely and wonderfully. But I saw that if a man or woman was genuinely turned to God for however long or short a time, even if it were for a single day of service given with an eternal intention, he should experience all three degrees of delight. The more the loving soul sees this courtesy of God, the more gladly will he serve him all the days of his life.

The seventh revelation: the recurring experience of delight and depression; it is good for man sometimes not to know comfort; it is not necessarily caused by sin

15 AFTER this he treated my soul to a supreme and spiritual pleasure. I was filled with an eternal assurance, which was powerfully maintained, without the least sort of grievous fear. This experience was so happy spiritually that I felt completely at peace and relaxed: nothing on earth could have disturbed me.

But this lasted only a short while and I began to react with a sense of loneliness and depression, and the futility of life; I was so tired of myself that I could scarcely bother to live. No comfort or relaxation now, just 'faith, hope, and charity'. And not much of these in feeling, but only in bare fact. Yet soon after this our blessed Lord gave once again that comfort and rest, so pleasant and sure, so delightful and powerful, that no fear, or sorrow, or physical suffering could have discomposed me. And then I felt the pain again; then the joy and pleasure; now it was one, and now the other, many times – I imagine quite twenty. When I was glad I was ready to say with St Paul, 'Nothing shall separate me from the love of Christ', and when I suffered, I could have said with St Peter, 'Lord, save me; I perish!'

I understood this vision to mean that it was for their own good that some souls should have this sort of experience: sometimes to be consoled; sometimes to be bereft and left to themselves. The will of God is that we should know he keeps us safely, alike 'in weal or woe'. For his own soul's good a man is sometimes left to himself. This is not invariably due to sin, for certainly I had not sinned when I was left alone – it happened all too suddenly. On the other hand I did not deserve to have this experience of blessedness. But our Lord gives it as and when he pleases, just as he sometimes permits us to know its opposite. Both are equally his love. For it is God's will that we should know the greatest happiness we are capable of, for this bliss is to last for ever. Suffering is transient for those who are to be saved, and will ultimately vanish completely. It is not God's will therefore that we should grieve and sorrow over our present sufferings, but rather that we should leave them at once, and keep ourselves in his everlasting joy.

The eighth revelation: the pitiful suffering of Christ as he dies, his discoloured face, and dried-up body

16 It was after this that Christ showed me something of his passion near the time of his dying. I saw his dear face, dry, bloodless, and pallid with death. It became more pale, deathly and lifeless. Then, dead, it turned a blue colour, gradually changing to a browny blue, as the flesh continued to die. For me his passion was shown primarily through his blessed face, and particularly by his lips. There too I saw these same four colours, though previously they had been, as I had seen, fresh, red, and lovely. It was a sorry business to see him change as he progressively died. His nostrils too shrivelled and dried before my eyes, and his dear body became black and

brown as it dried up in death; it was no longer its own fair, living colour.

For at the same time as our blessed Lord and Saviour was dying on the cross there was, in my picture of it, a strong, dry, and piercingly cold wind. Even when the precious blood was all drained from that dear body, there still remained a certain moisture in his flesh, as was shown me. The loss of blood and the pain within, the gale and the cold without, met together in his dear body. Between them the four (two outside, two in) with the passage of time dried up the flesh of Christ. The pain, sharp and bitter, lasted a very long time, and I could see it painfully drying up the natural vitality of his flesh. I saw his dear body gradually dry out, bit by bit, withering with dreadful suffering. And while there remained any natural vitality, so long he suffered pain. And it seemed to me, that with all this drawn-out pain, he had been a week in dying, dying and on the point of passing all that time he endured this final suffering. When I say 'it seemed to me that he had been a week in dying' I am only meaning that his dear body was so discoloured and dry, so shrivelled, deathly, and pitiful, that he might well have been seven nights in dying. And I thought to myself that the withering of his flesh was the severest part, as it was the last, of all Christ's passion.

The dreadful, physical thirst of Christ; the four reasons for this; his pitiful crowning; a lover's greatest pain

17 AND the words of Christ dying came to mind, 'I thirst.' I saw that he was thirsty in a twofold sense, physical and spiritual – of this latter I shall be speaking in the thirty-first chapter. The immediate purpose of this particular word was to stress the physical thirst, which I assumed to be caused by drying up of the moisture. For that blessed flesh and

frame was drained of all blood and moisture. Because of the pull of the nails and the weight of that blessed body it was a long time suffering. For I could see that the great, hard, hurtful nails in those dear and tender hands and feet caused the wounds to gape wide and the body to sag forward under its own weight, and because of the time it hung there. His head was scarred and torn, and the crown was sticking to it, congealed with blood; his dear hair and his withered flesh was entangled with the thorns, and they with it. At first, when the flesh was still fresh and bleeding the constant pressure of the thorns made the wounds even deeper. Furthermore, I could see that the dear skin and tender flesh, the hair and the blood, were hanging loose from the bone, gouged by the thorns in many places. It seemed about to drop off, heavy and loose, still holding its natural moisture, sagging like a cloth. The sight caused me dreadful and great grief; I would have died rather than see it fall off. What the cause of it was I could not see, but I assumed that it was due to the sharp thorns, and the rough and cruel way the garland was pressed home heartlessly and pitilessly. All this continued awhile, and then it began to change before my very eyes, and I marvelled. I saw that it was beginning to dry, and therefore to lose weight, and to congeal around the garland. And as it went right round the head, it made another garland under the first. The garland of thorns was dyed the colour of his blood, and this second garland of blood, and his head generally, were the colour of blood that is congealed and dry. What could be seen of the skin of the face was covered with tiny wrinkles, and was tan coloured; it was like a plank when it has been planed and dried out. The face was browner than the body.

The cause of dryness was fourfold: the first was caused by his bloodlessness; the second by the ensuing pain; the third by his hanging in the air, like some cloth hung out to dry; the fourth was due to his physical need of drink – and there was no comfort to relieve all his suffering and discomfort. Hard and grievous pain! But much harder and more grievous still when the moisture ceased, and all began to dry!

The pains experienced in that blessed head were these: the first was known in the act of dying, while the body was still moist, and the other was that killing, contracting drying which, with the strong wind blowing, shrivelled and hurt him with cold more than I could possibly imagine. And there were other pains beyond power to describe – for I recognize that whatever I might say about them would be quite inadequate.

This showing of Christ's pain filled me with pain myself. For though I was fully aware that he suffered only once, it seemed as if he wanted to show it all to me, and to fill my mind with it as indeed I had asked. All the while he was suffering I personally felt no pain but for him. And I thought to myself, 'I know but little of the pain that I asked for', and, wretch that I am, at once repented, thinking that had I known what it would have been I should have hesitated before making such a prayer. For my pains, I thought, passed beyond any physical death. Was there any pain like this? And my reason answered, 'Hell is a different pain, for there there is despair as well. But of all the pains that lead to salvation this is the greatest, to see your Love suffer. How could there be greater pain than to see him suffer, who is all my life, my bliss, my joy?' Here it was that I truly felt that I loved Christ so much more than myself, and that there could be no pain comparable to the sorrow caused by seeing him in pain.

CHAPTER EIGHTEEN

The spiritual martyrdom of our Lady, and others of Christ's lovers;
all things suffer with him, good and bad alike

18 BECAUSE of all this I was able to understand something of the compassion of our Lady St Mary. She and Christ were so one in their love that the greatness of her love caused the greatness of her suffering. In this I found an example of that instinctive love that creation has to him – and which develops by grace. This sort of love was most fully and supremely shown in his dear Mother. Just because she loved him more than did anyone else, so much the more did her sufferings transcend theirs. The higher, and greater, and sweeter our love, so much deeper will be our sorrow when we see the body of our beloved suffer. All his disciples and real lovers suffered more greatly here than at their own dying. I felt quite certain that the very least of them loved Christ much more than they loved themselves, and quite beyond my power to describe.

Here too I saw a close affinity between Christ and ourselves – at least, so I thought – for when he suffered, we suffered. All creatures capable of suffering pain suffered with him; I mean, all creatures that God has made for our use. Even heaven and earth languished for grief in their own peculiar way when Christ died. It is their nature to know him to be their God, from whom they draw all their powers. When he failed, then needs must that they too most properly should fail to the limit of their ability, grieving for his pains. So too his friends suffered pain because they loved him. Speaking generally we can say that all suffered, for even those who did not know him suffered when the normal conditions of life failed – though the mighty, secret keeping of God did not fail. I am thinking of two kinds of people, exemplified by two quite different types: Pilate, and St Denis of France, who at that time was a pagan.

When he saw the extraordinary and frightening portents of that day he said, 'Either the world is now at its end, or its Maker is suffering.' So he wrote upon an altar, 'This is the Altar of the Unknown God.' God in his goodness makes planets and the elements to work according to their nature for good and bad alike, but on that day it was withdrawn from both. So it was that even those who did not know him sorrowed at that time.

Thus was our Lord Jesus set at nought for us, and we too with him stand to suffer in a similar way, until such time as we come to his glory, as I shall explain later.

The comfort of looking at the crucifix; physical desire is not sin if the soul does not assent as well; the body will suffer until united to Christ

19 THERE were times when I wanted to look away from the cross, but I dared not. For I knew that while I gazed on the cross I was safe and sound, and I was not willingly going to imperil my soul. Apart from the cross there was no assurance against the horror of fiends. Then a friendly suggestion was put into my mind, 'Look up to heaven to his Father.' I saw clearly by the faith I had that there was nothing between the cross and heaven to distress me. I had either to look up or to reply. So I made inward answer as firmly as I could, and said, 'No. I cannot. You are my heaven.' I said this because I would not look. I would rather endure that suffering until the Day of Judgement than to come to heaven apart from him. I was quite clear that he who held me so closely bound could equally well release me when he pleased. Thus I was taught to choose Jesus for my heaven, whom I never at this time saw apart from his suffering. I wanted no other

heaven than Jesus, who will be my joy when I do eventually get there.

Ever since, this has been a great comfort to me that by his grace I chose Jesus for my heaven, and him in all his passion and grief. It taught me to choose only Jesus for my heaven, come what may. For, wretch that I was, I had already regretted having asked this favour. Had I known the sort of suffering it would involve, I should have thought twice about praying for it. But now I could recognize it for what it was: the natural demurring and reaction of the body. My soul was not protesting, nor was God blaming me. I was experiencing both regret and deliberate choice at one and the same time. And this was due to the two sides of our nature, outward and inward. The outward side is our mortal physical nature, which will continue to suffer and grieve all the time it lives – as I knew only too well! It was this part of me that regretted it all. The inward side is exalted and joyful and vital, all peaceful and loving. And deep down I was experiencing this. It was this part of me that so strongly, sensibly, and deliberately chose Jesus for my heaven. In this way I saw the truth that the inward part is superior to, and governor of, the outward, and that it was neither responsible for its desires, nor should it heed them, for its own intention is deliberately and eternally set on being united to our Lord Jesus. That the outward could draw the inward to conform to it was not shown me: rather was it shown that the inward should by grace draw the outward, that by the power of Christ both might be made eternally and blessedly one.

*The indescribable passion of Christ; three things about his passion
that we must always remember*

20 Thus it was that I saw our Lord Jesus languish a
long time. For the union in him of Godhead with
manhood strengthened the latter to suffer for love's sake more
than the whole of mankind could suffer. I mean, not only that
he suffered more pain than they, but that the pain he endured
for our salvation was more than the whole body of mankind
from the beginning to the end of time could experience or
imagine. We have only to contrast the worthiness of the most
high and revered king, with his shameful, scandalous, painful
death: he that is the most high and most worthy was the most
fully humiliated and most utterly despised. For the fundamental thing about the passion is to consider who he is who
has suffered. I began to think about the majesty and greatness of his glorious Godhead, now united with his precious,
tender, body; I also remembered how we creatures loathe
to suffer pain. For just as he was the gentlest and purest
of all, so too would the strength of his sufferings be greatest
of all.

He suffered for the sin of every one who is to be saved: and
seeing the sorrow and desolation of us all himself was made
sorry through his kindness and love. Just as our Lady grieved
for his suffering, so too he grieved for her sorrow – and more,
of course, since his own humanity was by its nature more
worthy. All the time he could suffer, he did suffer for us, and
sorrow too. Now that he is risen and is impassible, he still
suffers with us.

By his grace I saw all this, and saw that the love which he
had for our soul was so strong that he chose to suffer quite
deliberately and with strong desire, enduring what he did with
meekness and long-suffering. For when a soul that is touched

94

by grace can see it in this way, it sees indeed that the pains of Christ's passion surpass all our pains; that is to say, all those pains which, by virtue of that passion, will be turned into supreme and eternal joys.

Three ways of looking at Christ's passion; dying on the cross with Christ; his look banishes pain

21 As I understand it, it is God's will for us to look at our Lord's passion in three different ways. And the first is to see with contrition and compassion the severe pain he experienced. That was shown me by our Lord at this time, and by his grace I was enabled so to see it.

I looked with all my might for the moment of his dying, and thought I would have seen his body completely dead. But I did not see him thus. And just as I was thinking that his life was about to finish and that I must be shown his end, suddenly, while I gazed on the cross, his expression changed to cheerful joy! The change in his blessed countenance changed mine too, and I was as glad and happy as could be. Then our Lord put this thought in my mind, 'What point is there in your pain and grief, now?' And I was happy indeed. I understood him to mean that we, through our own pains and passion, are now dying with him on his cross, and that as we deliberately abide on that same cross, helped by his grace, to the very end, suddenly his expression shall change, and we shall be with him in heaven. Between the one thing and the other no time shall intervene: all shall be brought to joy. This is what he meant by this revelation, 'What point is there in your pain and grief now?' We shall be blessed indeed!

I saw perfectly clearly that if he was going to show us *now* his joy and gladness there can be no pain, earthly or otherwise, that will trouble us, but that all things should bring joy and gladness. But because he shows it along with his cross and passion (as he had to endure it in this life), so we too must endure discomfort and hardship with him – as indeed our natural weakness necessitates. He suffers because it is his will and goodness to raise us even higher in bliss. In exchange for the little that we have to suffer here, we shall have the supreme unending knowledge of God which we should never have without it. The sharper our suffering with him on his cross, the greater our glory with him in his kingdom.

The ninth revelation: the sight of three heavens; the infinite love of Christ who would be willing to suffer for us every day if necessary

22 THEN our good Lord Jesus Christ said, 'Are you well satisfied with my suffering for you?' 'Yes, thank you, good Lord,' I replied. 'Yes, good Lord, bless you.' And the kind Lord Jesus said, 'If you are satisfied, I am satisfied too. It gives me great happiness and joy and, indeed, eternal delight ever to have suffered for you. If I could possibly have suffered more, I would have done so.'

This experience lifted my mind to heaven, and I saw there to my amazement three heavens. And in the three heavens of my vision – all contained in the blessed humanity of Christ – no one of them is greater or less, higher or lower than the other, but each one is equally blessed.

The first heaven that Christ showed was his Father, not in any physical representation but as he is in his nature and mode of working; that is to say I saw in Christ what the Father is like. The Father works like this: he rewards his Son, Jesus Christ. This reward causes our Lord such happiness, that there is no other gift he would prefer to it. The first heaven is this pleasing of his Father – it was showed to me as a 'heaven', and as indeed blessed. For he is delighted with all that Jesus has done for our salvation. We belong to our Lord not only because he bought us, but because we are his Father's kindly gift: we are his joy, his reward, his glory, his crown. It is a unique thought (and delightful) that we should be his crown. And what I am saying is so great a joy to him that he counts as nothing his agony and passion, his cruel and shameful death.

In his word 'If I could possibly have suffered more, I would have done so' I saw that he would have died again and again, for his love would have given him no rest until he had done so. I was most attentive to discover how often he might have died. The number, indeed, was so far beyond my comprehension and knowledge that I was unable to count it. Yet all this potential dying he would count as nothing for love of us. In comparison with this it seemed a small matter.

For though the dear humanity of Christ could only suffer once, his goodness would always make him willing to do so – every day if need be. If he were to say that for love of me he would make a new heaven and a new earth, this would be a comparatively simple matter; something he could do every day if he wanted, with no great effort. But for love of me to be willing to die times without number – beyond human capacity to compute – is, to my mind, the greatest gesture our Lord God could make to the soul of man. This is his meaning: 'How could I not, out of love for you, do all I can for you? This would not be difficult, since for love of you I am ready to die often, regardless of the suffering.'

And here, for the second part of my threefold vision of the passion, I saw that the love which made him suffer is as much greater than his pain as heaven is greater than earth. For his suffering was a noble and most worthy deed worked out by love in time – and his love has no beginning, but is now, and ever shall be. It was because of this love he said, 'If I could possibly have suffered more, I would have done so.' He did *not* say 'If it were necessary to have suffered more.' Though it were not necessary, yet if he could suffer more, he would do so. This deed and this work for our salvation was ordered as well as God himself was able to order it. And I saw Christ's complete happiness; his happiness would not have been complete if it were at all possible to have done it better.

Christ wants us to rejoice with him over our redemption, and to seek his grace to do so

23 IN these three words, 'joy, happiness, and eternal delight', I was shown three heavens. By 'joy' I understood the pleasure experienced by the Father; 'happiness', the work of the Son; 'eternal delight', the Holy Spirit. The Father is pleased, the Son is worshipped, the Holy Spirit is delighted.

And here I saw the last part of my threefold vision of his passion, the joy and happiness that delighted him. For our Lord, in his courtesy, showed me his passion in five different ways: (i) the bleeding of his head; (ii) the discolouration of his face; (iii) the copious bleeding of the body – the result of the scourging; (iv) the depth of his dying. All these are what he suffered in his passion, so he then showed me (v) the joy and happiness of the passion.

It is the will of God that we too should delight with him in our salvation, and thereby be greatly comforted and strengthened. And his will is that our soul should cheerfully occupy itself with this fact, helped on by his grace. For we are his happiness: in us he ever delights; so too may we in him, aided by his grace. All that he has done for us, or is doing or will do, is at no cost to himself, his work for us in his humanity only excepted. And this began at his incarnation, and continued until his blessed resurrection on Easter Day. For that length of time did he pay the price of our redemption: a deed which causes him ceaseless pleasure, as I have said.

It is the will of Jesus that we should think carefully of the happiness of the Blessed Trinity over our salvation, so that we too, by his grace, should desire to have equal happiness. I mean, that as far as we can manage it, our delight in our salvation should be like Christ's. The whole Trinity was involved in the passion of Christ, giving us an abundance of virtue and grace by him, though only the Maiden's Son suffered. And because of this the whole Trinity rejoices eternally. This is shown by the words, 'Are you well satisfied?' and by the other words, 'If you are satisfied, I am satisfied too.' As if he were saying, 'It is sufficient joy and delight for me to know that I can truly satisfy you. I ask you nothing else as the result of my suffering.'

In this way he caused me to think about the essence of giving cheerfully. One who gives gladly pays little heed to what he is giving. All his desire and intention is to please and comfort the one to whom he gives it. And if the recipient accepts the gift gladly and gratefully, the gracious donor ignores the cost and pain of the gift to himself for delight and joy that he has pleased and comforted one whom he loves. This was shown me absolutely plainly.

Ponder carefully the range of this word *ever*. It describes the height of the love Christ knew for our salvation, and the manifold joys that flow from the passion. For example, he rejoices that the deed is past and done, and he shall suffer no more; he rejoices too that he has raised us to heaven, and made us to be his crown and eternal delight; again, he rejoices that by his passion he has bought us out from the eternal pain of hell.

The tenth revelation: our Lord Jesus rejoices to display in his love his blessed heart, riven in two

24 WITH a glad countenance our Lord looked at his side, rejoicing as he gazed. And as he looked, I, with my limited understanding, was led by way of this same wound into his side. There he showed me a place, fair and delightful, large enough for all saved mankind to rest in peace and love. I was reminded of the most precious blood and water that he shed for love of us. And, gazing still, he showed me his blessed heart riven in two. In his sweet enjoyment he helped me to understand, in part at any rate, how the blessed Godhead was moving the poor soul to appreciate the eternal love of God that has neither beginning nor end. At the same time our good Lord said, most blessedly, 'See, how I have loved you.' As if to say, 'My dearest, look at your Lord, your God, your Maker, and your endless joy. See the delight and happiness I have in your salvation; and because you love me, rejoice with me.'

For my greater understanding was this blessed word said, 'See how I have loved you.' It was as though he were saying, 'Behold and see that I have loved you so much that before I did actually die for you I *would* have died for you. And now I *have* died for you, and have willingly suffered all that I could. Now, all my bitter pain and mighty work has turned to my eternal happiness and joy – and to yours. How can you pray then for anything that delights me, and I not most gladly give it you? For my delight is in your holiness and in the endless joy and happiness you share with me.'

Put as simply as I can, this is how I understand this blessed word, 'See how I have loved you.' The good Lord showed me this to make us glad and cheerful.

CHAPTER TWENTY-FIVE

The eleventh revelation: a high and spiritual revelation of his Mother

25 AND with the same cheerful joy our good Lord looked down to his right and thereby brought to mind the place where our Lady was standing during his passion. 'Do you want to see her?' he said, saying in effect, 'I know quite well you want to see my blessed Mother, for, after myself, she is the greatest joy I can show you, and most like me and worthy of me. Of all my creation, she is the most desirable sight.' And because of his great, wonderful, unique love for this sweet maiden, his blessed Mother our Lady St Mary, he showed her to be rejoicing greatly. This was the meaning of these sweet words. It was as if he were saying, 'Do you want to see how I love her, so that you can rejoice with me in my love for her, and hers for me?'

Here – to understand this word further – our Lord God is speaking to all who are going to be saved, as it were to all mankind in the person of one individual. He is saying, 'Can you see in her how greatly you are loved? For love of you I made her so exalted, so noble, so worthy. This pleases me, and I want it to please you too.' For after himself she is the most blessed of all sights.

But, for all that, I am not expected to want to see her physically present here on earth, but rather to see the virtues of her blessed soul, her truth, her wisdom, her charity, so that I can learn to know myself, and reverently fear my God.

When our good Lord had showed me this and said, 'Do you want to see her?' I answered, 'Yes, good Lord, thank you very much. Yes, good Lord, if it is your will.' I prayed this often, and I thought I was going to see her in person. But I did not see her in this way. Jesus, in that word, gave me a spiritual sight of her. Just as I had seen her before, lowly and unaffected, so now he showed her, exalted, noble, glorious, and pleasing to him above all creation.

He wills it to be known that all who delight in him should delight in her too, with the same pleasure he has in her, and she in him. To help understand it better he gave this example. If a man loves one particular thing above everything else, he will try to make everyone else love and like what it is he loves so greatly. When Jesus said, 'Do you want to see her?' I thought it was the nicest word about her that he could possibly have said, together with the spiritual revelation that he gave me of her. Except in the case of our Lady, St Mary, our Lord showed me no one specially – and her he showed three times. The first occasion was when she was with child, the second sorrowing under the cross, and the third as she is now, delightful, glorious, and rejoicing.

The twelfth revelation: the Lord our God is the being of all that is, and supreme

26 AFTER this our Lord showed himself, in glory even greater than I had seen before – so it seemed to me. By this I was taught that our soul can never rest until it comes to him, and knows him to be fullness of joy, friendly and considerate, blessed and life indeed. And he said again and again 'It is I; it is I; it is I who am most exalted; it is I whom you love; it is I whom you delight in; it is I whom you serve; it is I whom you long for, whom you desire; it is I whom you mean; it is I who am all. It is I whom Holy Church preaches and teaches; it is I who showed myself to you here.'

The extent of what he had to say was altogether beyond my capacity to understand or take in. As I see it, his words are the greatest that can be uttered, for they embrace . . . I cannot tell! All I know is that the joy I saw in that revelation surpasses all the heart could wish for or the soul desire. So let not those words be recorded here, but let each receive them as our Lord intended them, according to the grace God gives him for understanding and loving.

The thirteenth revelation: God's will is that we should greatly value all his works; the noble nature of all creation; sin is known by suffering

27 AFTER this our Lord brought to mind the longing I had for him earlier. I now saw that nothing hindered me but sin. And this I saw to be true in general of us all and I thought to myself that if there had been no sin we should all have been clean and like our Lord, as when we were made. In my foolish way I had often wondered why the foreseeing wisdom of God could not have prevented the beginning of sin, for then, thought I, all would have been well. This line of thought ought to have been left well alone; as it was I grieved and sorrowed over it, with neither cause nor justification. But Jesus, who in this vision informed me of all I needed, answered, 'Sin was necessary – but it is all going to be all right; it is all going to be all right; everything is going to be all right.' In this simple word *sin* our Lord reminded me in a general sort of way of all that is not good: the despicable shame and utter self-denial he endured for us, both in his life and in his dying. And of all the suffering and pain of his creation, both spiritual and physical. For all of us have already experienced something of this abnegation and we have to deny ourselves as we follow our master, Jesus, until we are wholly cleansed. I mean, until this body of death and our inward affections (which are not very good) are completely done away. All this I saw, together with all the suffering that ever has been or can be. And of all

pain I understood that the passion of Christ was the greatest and most surpassing. All this was shown in a flash, and quickly passed over into consolation – for our good Lord would not have the soul frightened by this ugly sight.

But I did not see *sin*. I believe it has no substance or real existence. It can only be known by the pain it causes. This pain is something, as I see it, which lasts but a while. It purges us and makes us know ourselves, so that we ask for mercy. The passion of our Lord is our comfort against all this – for such is his blessed will. Because of his tender love for all those who are to be saved our good Lord comforts us at once and sweetly, as if to say, 'It is true that sin is the cause of all this pain; but it is all going to be all right; it is all going to be all right; everything is going to be all right.' These words were said most tenderly, with never a hint of blame either to me or to any of those to be saved. It would be most improper of me therefore to blame or criticize God for my sin, since he does not blame me for it.

In these words I saw one of God's marvellously deep secrets – a secret which he will plainly reveal to us in heaven. And when we know it we will see the reason why he allowed sin to come, and seeing, we shall rejoice in him for ever.

The heirs of salvation are shaken by sorrow; Christ rejoices in his compassion; a remedy for trouble

28 IN this way I saw how Christ has compassion upon us because of our sin. And just as previously I had been full of sorrow and compassion at the sight of his suffering, so now I was filled with compassion for all my fellow Christians, those people greatly beloved and saved, the servants of God. For Holy Church shall be shaken at the world's sorrow, anguish, and tribulation, just as men shake a cloth in the wind.

Our Lord gave me an answer about all this. 'I shall make of this a great thing in heaven – a thing of everlasting worth and endless joy.' I could now understand how our Lord rejoiced in the tribulations of his servants, though with pity and compassion. To bring them to bliss he lays on each one he loves some particular thing, which while it carries no blame in his sight causes them to be blamed by the world, despised, scorned, mocked, and rejected. This he does to forestall any hurt they might get from the pomps and vanities of this sinful world, to prepare their way to heaven, and to exalt them in his everlasting bliss. For he says, 'I shall wholly break you of your empty affections and your pernicious pride. Then I shall gather you together, and by uniting you to myself make you humble and mild, clean and holy.' Then it was that I saw that all the kind compassion and love a man may have for his fellow Christian is due to the fact that Christ is in him.

The same total abnegation shown in his passion was shown again here in this compassion. The significance is twofold: there is the bliss to which we are brought, the enjoyment that is in him; and there is the comfort we may have in our suffering. He wants us to know that all this will be changed into glory and profit through his passion; to know, moreover, that we do not suffer on our own, but with him; to see in him the ground of our being; to recognize that his suffering and self-abnegation so far surpasses anything we might experience that we shall never wholly understand it.

To see this will stop us from moaning and despairing about our own sufferings. We can see that our sin well deserves it, but that his love excuses us. In his great courtesy he overlooks the blame, and regards us with sympathy and pity, children both innocent and loved.

*Adam's was the greatest sin; its reparation is more pleasing to God
than ever the sin was harmful*

29 BUT while I understood all this I was still troubled and
grieved, and said to our Lord (and I meant it with
great fear), 'Good Lord, how can everything be all right
when such great hurt has come to your creatures through sin?'
I desired, as far as I dared, to have more information for my
own peace of mind. This our blessed Lord answered most
humbly and cheerfully, showing me that the greatest wrong
ever done was Adam's sin. This, moreover, is clearly recognized throughout Holy Church on earth. Furthermore he
taught me that I should see the glorious reparation, for this
making of amends is incomparably more pleasing and honouring to God than ever was the sin of Adam harmful. The
meaning of our blessed Lord was this, 'Since I have now made
the greatest wrong good, I want you to know by this that I
shall make good all wrongs of whatever degree.'

*We are to rejoice and trust in our Saviour, Jesus; we are not to pry
into his secrets*

30 HE gave me to understand that in these things there
were two parts. One part concerns our Saviour and
our salvation. There is no mystery about this part – it is clear,
beautiful, splendid, and abundant. Everyone of present and
future goodwill is included in it. To it we are bound, and to it
we are drawn by God; in it are we advised, and in it are we
instructed, inwardly by the Holy Spirit, and outwardly
through the same grace by Holy Church. In this our Lord
intends us to be occupied: delighting in himself, as he delights

in us. The more fully we make this truth our own, with reverent humility, the more thanks we get from him, and greater gain for ourselves. Thus, so to speak, do we enjoy our share of our Lord.

The other part is completely hidden from us, for it deals with all those things that do not concern our salvation. It is our Lord's own private matter, and it is the royal prerogative of God to be undisturbed in that which is his own business. It is not for his servant, obedient and reverent, to pry at all into these secrets. True, our Lord has pity and compassion on those of us who busy ourselves therewith. Yet I am sure that if we realized how much it would please him and benefit ourselves to refrain from this, we would stop. The desire of the saints in heaven is only to know such things as our Lord wills to show them. Their love and their longing likewise are ruled by the Lord's will. And this ought to be *our* will too, like theirs. Then should we want and desire nothing but the Lord's will, just as they do. For in God's purpose they and we are to be the same.

Here it was that I was taught to trust and rejoice only in our blessed Saviour, Jesus, and in whatever circumstances.

Christ's spiritual longing and thirst, which lasts till the Day of Judgement; because of his body he is not yet fully glorified or impassible

31 THUS our good Lord answered all the questions and doubts that I could produce. Most reassuringly he added, 'I may make everything all right; I am able to; I intend to, and I shall. You will see for yourself that every sort of thing will be all right.'

When he says 'I may', I understand it to refer to the Father; when he says 'I am able to', to the Son; when he says 'I intend to', it is the Holy Spirit; when he says 'I shall', it means the blessed Trinity in Unity – three Persons and one truth; when he says 'You will see for yourself', the union of all saved mankind with the blessed Trinity is intended. In these five words God wills that we be enfolded – in rest and peace.

Thus shall the spiritual thirst of Christ be quenched. This is his thirst: his love and longing for us that goes on enduring until we see the Day of Judgement. For of us who are to be saved and be Christ's joy and bliss some are alive now, while others are yet unborn; and so it will go on until that Day. His thirst and loving longing is to have us all, integrated in him, to his great enjoyment. At least, so I see it. We are not as fully whole in him now as we shall be then. We know by our creed, and it was made clear in the revelations, that Jesus Christ is both God and man. Because he is God he is supreme blessedness, and never has been nor ever shall be other. His eternal blessedness can neither be increased nor diminished. This was made abundantly clear in the revelations, and particularly in the twelfth, where he says, 'It is I who am most exalted.' Because he is human – this too is known by the creed, and by the revelations – it was shown that he, though God, suffered pain, passion, and death, for love of us and to bring us to blessedness. In this work of his humanity he rejoices. He showed this in the ninth revelation when he said, 'It gives me joy, happiness, and eternal delight ever to have suffered for you.' This is what makes his work so happy, and this is his meaning when in the same revelation he says that 'we are his joy, his reward, his glory, his crown'.

Since Christ is our Head, he must be both glorious and impassible. But since he is also the Body in which all his members are joined he is not yet fully either of these. Therefore the same desire and thirst that he had upon the cross – and this desire, longing, and thirst was with him from the very first, I fancy – he has still, and shall continue to have until the last soul to be saved has arrived at its blessedness. For just as there is in God the quality of sympathy and pity, so too in him is there that of thirst and longing. And in virtue of this longing which is in Christ we in turn long for him too. No soul comes to heaven without it. This quality of longing and thirst springs from God's eternal goodness just as pity does. Though, to my mind, longing and pity are quite distinct, it is the same goodness that gives point to the spiritual thirst; a thirst which persists in him as long as we are in need, and which draws us up to his blessedness. All this was seen in the revelation of his compassion. It shall cease on the Day of Judgement.

Thus does he have pity and compassion upon us, and he longs to possess us. But his wisdom and love will not allow the end to come before the time is right.

Everything will be well, and Scripture fulfilled; it is the will of Christ that we keep ourselves steadfastly in the Faith of Holy Church

32 ON one occasion the good Lord said, 'Everything is going to be all right.' On another, 'You will see for yourself that every sort of thing will be all right.' In these two sayings the soul discerns various meanings.

One is that he wants us to know that not only does he care for great and noble things, but equally for little and small, lowly and simple things as well. This is his meaning: '*Everything will be all right.*' We are to know that the least thing will not be forgotten.

Another is this: we see deeds done that are so evil, and injuries inflicted that are so great, that it seems to us quite impossible that any good can come of them. As we consider these, sorrowfully and mournfully, we cannot relax in the blessed contemplation of God as we ought. This is caused by the fact that our reason is now so blind, base, and ignorant that we are unable to know that supreme and marvellous wisdom, might, and goodness which belong to the blessed Trinity. This is the meaning of his word, 'You will see for yourself that every *sort* of thing will be all right.' It is as if he were saying, 'Be careful now to believe and trust, and in the end you will see it all in its fullness and joy.'

So from those same six words 'I may make everything all right', I gain great comfort with regard to all the works that God has still to do. There still remains a deed which the blessed Trinity will do at the last Day – at least so I see it – yet when and how it will be done is unknown to all God's creatures under Christ, and will remain so until it takes place. The reason why he wants us to know about this deed is that he would have us more at ease in our minds and more at peace in our love, and not be concerned with those storms and stresses that stop us from truly enjoying him.

This great deed, ordained by the Lord God from before time, and treasured and hid within his blessed heart, is known only to himself. By it he will make everything to turn out well. For just as the blessed Trinity made everything out of nothing, in the same way shall he make all that is wrong to turn out for the best.

The consideration of this I found most marvellous, and in my wonder I thought about our faith: our faith is grounded in God's word, and part of it is that we who believe in that word of God will be saved – completely. Another part of our same belief is that many creatures will be damned; for example, the angels who fell from heaven through pride, and are now fiends; and those men on earth who die apart from the Faith of Holy Church, namely, the heathen; and those too, who are christened but live unchristian lives, and so die out of love – all these shall be condemned to hell everlastingly, as Holy Church teaches me to believe. This being so I thought it quite impossible that everything should turn out well, as our Lord was now showing me. But I had no answer to this revelation save this: 'What is impossible to you is not impossible to me. I shall honour my word in every respect, and I will make everything turn out for the best.' Thus was I taught by God's grace to hold steadfastly to the faith I had already learned, and at the same time to believe quite seriously that everything *would* turn out all right, as our Lord was showing. For the great deed that our Lord is going to do is that by which he shall keep his word in every particular, and make all that is wrong turn out well. How this will be no one less than Christ can know – not until the deed is done. At least, this is what I understood our Lord to mean at the time.

All damned souls are despised in the sight of God, as is the Devil; these revelations are not counter to the Faith of Holy Church, but support it; the busier we are about God's secrets, the less we know

33 YET in all this I wanted (as far as I dared) to get a real sight of hell and purgatory. It was not my intention, of course, to put any article of the Faith to the test, for I steadfastly believed that hell and purgatory existed for the same end that Holy Church taught. What I was hoping for however was to see (and thereby to learn) those things that are taught by the Faith, and so to live more worthily of God and more profitably to myself. But for all my desire I saw absolutely nothing, except what was said earlier in the fifth revelation where I saw the devil reproved by God and condemned eternally. By this I gathered that all creatures who are of the devil's sort and die as such are no more mentioned before God and his holy ones, any more than the devil is himself, notwithstanding they are human beings, and christened maybe.

For though the revelation was one of goodness, with very little reference to evil, I was not drawn thereby from any article of the Faith in which Holy Church teaches me to believe. For I had had a sight of the passion of Christ in various revelations (the first, second, fifth, and eighth, as I have already said) and had in some way shared the experience of our Lady's sorrow and of those true friends who saw him suffer. Even there I did not see the Jews specifically mentioned as those who did him to death. By my Faith I knew that they were accursed and eternally damned, except those, of course, who had been converted by grace. The general result was that I was strengthened and taught to keep myself in every article of the Faith, and in what I had learned previously, and to hope that God's mercy and grace were still with me. And there was an inner desire and prayer to continue thus unto the end of my life.

It is God's will for us to pay great attention to all his past acts, but always to leave on one side speculation as to the last great deed. We should want to be like our brethren, the saints in heaven, who will nothing but God's will: only then shall we rejoice in God, and be content whether he conceals or reveals. For I saw this truth in our Lord's meaning: the busier we are about discovering his secrets in this matter or that, the farther we shall be from their discovery.

God shows his lovers such secrets as they need to know; those who receive the Church's teaching with sincerity please him

34 OUR Lord showed secrets of two kinds. One is this great secret on which all other secrets depend. His will is that we recognize these to be hidden until such time as he declares them. The other consists of those secrets he is willing to reveal and make known. His will is for us to know that it is

his will that we should know them! They are secrets not merely because that is his will, but because we are blind and ignorant. This he greatly pities, and accordingly himself opens them up to us, so that we may know him thereby and love and cling to him. All we need to know and understand our Lord will most graciously show us, both by this means and by the preaching and teaching of Holy Church. God has shown the very great pleasure given him by all those men and women who wholeheartedly, humbly and willingly, receive the preaching and teaching of Holy Church. For it is *his* Holy Church. He is its foundation, its being, its teaching. He is its teacher, and the end and the reward for which every normal soul is striving. This is known and shall be known by every soul to whom the Holy Spirit declares it. And I hope indeed that all those who seek this he will speed on their way: for they seek God.

All I have said so far, and all that I am going to say, is a comfort against sin. In the third revelation when I saw that God does everything I saw no sin, and I saw that everything was all right. But it was when God showed me sin that he said, 'Everything is going to be all right.'

God does everything that is good; he permits everything by his
mercy and for his glory; these will shine forth when sin is no
longer permitted

35 SINCE Almighty God had shown his goodness so generously and fully I was anxious to learn whether a certain person I loved would continue living the good life which I hoped had been begun. But this particular desire seemed to hinder me, for I received no reply whatever. And then my reason, just as a friend would, supplied the answer. 'Interpret it generally, and be mindful of the courtesy of the

Lord in showing it at all. It is more honouring to God to see him in everything than in any particular thing.' I agreed, and so I learned that it was more honouring to God to see him in all things generally than to concentrate on any one thing in particular. If I were wise enough to act on this advice I should not be made glad by anything specially, nor on the other hand should I be much distressed by anything else, for 'Everything will be all right.' The fullness of joy is to see God in all things.

To the same blessed power, wisdom, and love by which he made them are all things being continually led, and our Lord himself will bring them there. In due time we shall see. The reason for this was shown in the first revelation, and more clearly in the third where it was said, 'I saw the whole Godhead concentrated in a single point.'

All our Lord does is right, and what he permits is worthwhile. These two definitions embrace both good and evil, for all that is good is done by our Lord, and all that is evil is permitted by him. I am not admitting of course that evil has any worth. I am merely saying that our Lord's tolerance of it has, for in this way his goodness is always known in its wonderful humility and gentleness; and that because of his mercy and grace.

That thing is right which is so good that it cannot be better. God himself is true righteousness and all his works are rightly done, for they were ordained before time by his supreme might, wisdom, and goodness. Just as he has ordained them to be the best possible, so too he works continually to achieve this same end. He is always completely satisfied with himself and his works. The sight of this blessed harmony is sweet indeed to the soul who can see by grace. All souls who are to be saved eternally are, by his goodness, made righteous in the sight of God. And in this righteousness we, above all else, are kept eternally and wonderfully.

Mercy is the work of God's goodness, and will continue to

work as long as sin is allowed to harry righteous souls. When sin is given leave no longer, then too shall the work of mercy cease. All will have been brought to righteousness, and will remain so for ever. By his permission we fall: and by his blessed love, power, and wisdom we are kept – and by his merciful grace we are raised to many, many more joys. So for his righteousness and mercy he intends to be known and loved now and for ever. And the soul that by grace wisely considers this is well satisfied with both, and delights in them for ever.

Another splendid deed of our Lord; it may partly be understood here below for our rejoicing; God still works miracles

36 Our Lord God showed me that he was going to perform this deed, and were I to do nothing but sin, my sin would still not prevent his goodness from working. I saw that the recognition of this fact brought a heavenly joy to the Godfearing soul who, by his kind grace, desired to do his will. The deed will begin here on earth, and it will be worthy of God, and abundantly beneficial to his lovers. As soon as we reach heaven we shall behold it with marvelling joy, and so it will work out till the Last Day. For ever shall its worth and blessedness endure in heaven before God and his holy ones.

Such was the significance and meaning given it by our Lord. And he showed it in order to make us rejoice in him and all his works. When I saw that his revelation was continuing, I understood that it was shown because of the greatness of this coming event. God was revealing that he himself would do it: this deed with all those qualities already mentioned. All this he showed to my great delight, meaning me to take it wisely, faithfully, and trustfully. But what his deed was going to be was kept secret from me.

In this way I saw that he wished us not to be afraid of knowing such things as he might show us. He shows them because he wants us to know them. By this knowing he would have us love him, rejoice in him, and enjoy him for ever. Because of his great love he shows us everything that is worthwhile and beneficial for the time. The very things that he now keeps secret are shown by his great goodness to be secret. This shows that he wants us to believe and understand that we shall see them revealed in his eternal blessedness. We ought to rejoice in him then, both for what he shows and for what he hides! And if we deliberately and humbly do this we shall experience great relief – and earn his eternal gratitude.

This is the significance of his word: it shall be done for me (which means mankind in general: in other words, all who are to be saved), and will be at once worthwhile, wonderful, and abundant; and God himself will do it. This will be the most wonderful joy imaginable, to see the deed that God himself shall do, while man can do no better than sin! Our Lord God means in as many words, 'Look! Here you have material for humility, for love, for total self denial, for enjoying me. Because I love you, enjoy me! This will please me most of all.' While we live, whenever in our folly we turn to contemplate what is forbidden, our Lord God, in his blessed tenderness, with a touch calls us, speaking in our soul, 'Let go what you are loving, dearest child. Mean me. I am all you want. Rejoice in your Saviour and your salvation.' That this is our Lord's work in us I am sure. The soul, perceptive by grace, will appreciate this. Though it is true that this deed refers to man in general, the particular individual is not thereby excluded. What our Lord will intend for his poor creatures I do not yet know. But this and the deed mentioned earlier are not one and the same, but quite distinct. The one we have just been talking about will happen as soon as each of us gets to heaven. And, if our Lord allows, we may know something about it here. But the great deed spoken of earlier will not be known till it is done – either by heaven or earth.

Moreover God gave me special insight and instruction about miracles: 'It is known that I have done miracles here in the past; many, marvellous, estimable, and great. What I did then, I do still, and shall continue to do.' We know that before a miracle happens there is sorrow, distress, trouble. This reminds us of our weakness, and the mischief that our falling into sin causes. So we humble ourselves, and fear God, crying for his help and grace. Miracles follow; and they come through the supreme power, wisdom, and goodness of God; they demonstrate his virtue and the joys of heaven as far as may be in this passing life. Thus our faith is strengthened, and our hope increased in love. And this is the reason why God is pleased to be known and honoured by miracles. He means that we should not be too cast down because of the sorrow and storms that beset us: it is always like this before miracles!

God keeps his elect securely, although they sin; there is in them a godly will that never consents to sin

37 GOD reminded me that I would sin. But because I was so enjoying looking at him I did not pay much attention to this revelation, and our Lord most mercifully bided my time, and gave me grace to attend. This revelation I appropriated to myself personally, but by all the gracious comfort that followed I was taught to apply it – as you shall see – to all my fellow Christians, considered generally and not particularly. Though our Lord showed that *I* would sin, *I* here stands for *all*. Because of this I began to be rather fearful. And our Lord answered 'I am keeping you very securely.' The word was said with more love and assurance and a sense of spiritual protection than I know how to tell. For just as I had

been shown that I was likely to sin, so at the same time was I comforted with assurance and protection for all my fellow Christians. What can make me love my fellow Christians more than to see in God that he loves all who are to be saved as if they were one soul?

In every soul to be saved is a godly will that has never consented to sin, in the past or in the future. Just as there is an animal will in our lower nature that does not will what is good, so there is a godly will in our higher part, which by its basic goodness never wills what is evil, but only what is good. This is the reason why he loves us, and why we can always do what pleases him.

This truth our Lord made evident when he revealed the complete love in which he sees us to stand. Yes indeed, he loves us as much here as he will do there when we stand before his blessed face. Our primary concern is to see that *our* love does not fail.

The sins of the elect are changed into matters of rejoicing and glory; examples are found in King David, St Peter, and St John of Beverley

38 MOREOVER God showed that sin need be no shame to a man but can even be worthwhile. For just as every sin has its corresponding penalty because God is true, so the same soul can know every sin to have its corresponding blessing because God is love. Just as various sins are punished with various penalties according to their seriousness, so may they be rewarded with various joys in heaven if they have brought punishment and sorrow to the soul on earth. For the soul that comes to heaven is precious to God, and the place is so holy that the goodness of God will never allow the soul who gets there to have sinned without that sin being

compensated. Ever known, it is blessedly made good by God's surpassing worth.

In this vision my mind was lifted up to heaven, and God cheered me by reminding me of David and countless others in the Old Testament, and of Mary Magdalen, Peter and Paul, and Thomas, in the New; and of St John of Beverley and numberless others. He reminded me how the church on earth knows them to have been sinners, yet they are not despised for that reason, but rather these things have in some way turned out to their honour. The courtesy our Lord shows them here reflects in part what he will show them there in full. For there what sin typifies is changed to a thing of honour.

St John of Beverley our Lord showed vividly, a comfort to us because he was so homely and unaffected, which brought to mind the fact that he was a near neighbour and acquaintance. God called him, most happily, 'St John of Beverley' just as we do, showing that he sees him as an exalted saint in heaven, and blessed. At the same time he mentioned that in his young and tender years he was a very dear servant of God, loving and fearing God very greatly. Yet God allowed him to fall, though in his mercy he kept him from perishing, and from losing ground. Afterwards God raised him to much greater grace, and because of the humility and contrition of his life, in heaven God has given him many joys, greater even than those he would have had had he never fallen. And God shows this to be true by the many and continuing miracles that are wrought by his body today. All this makes us glad and cheerful and loving.

The sharpness of sin; the goodness of contrition; our kind Lord
does not wish us to despair over our frequent falls

39 Sin is the sharpest scourge that any elect soul can be flogged with. It is the scourge which so reduces a man or woman and makes him loathsome in his own sight that it is not long before he thinks himself fit only to sink down to hell . . . until the touch of the Holy Spirit forces him to contrition, and turns his bitterness to the hope of God's mercy. Then he begins to heal his wounds, and to rouse his soul as it turns to the life of Holy Church. The Holy Spirit leads him on to confession, so that he deliberately reveals his sins in all their nakedness and reality, and admits with great sorrow and shame that he has befouled the fair image of God. Then for all his sins he performs penance imposed by his confession according to the doctrine of Holy Church, and the teaching of the Holy Spirit. This is one of the humble things that greatly pleases God. Physical illness that is sent by him is another. Others are those humiliations and griefs caused by outside influences, or by the rejection and contempt of the world, or by the various kinds of difficulty and temptation a man may find himself in, whether they be physical or spiritual.

Dearly indeed does our Lord hold on to us when it seems to us that we are nearly forsaken and cast away because of our sin – and deservedly so. Because of the humility we acquire this way we are exalted in the sight of God by his grace, and know a very deep contrition and compassion and a genuine longing for God. Then suddenly we are delivered from sin and pain, and raised to blessedness and even made great saints!

By contrition we are made clean; by compassion, ready; and by a genuine longing for God, worthy. It is by means of these three that souls can attain heaven, as I understand it. (I am referring, of course, to those who were sinners on earth, and who are to be saved.) By these medicines it is necessary for every soul to be healed. Though healed, the soul's wounds are still seen by God, not as wounds, but as honourable scars. Counterbalancing our punishment here with its sorrow and penance is our reward in heaven through the courteous love of almighty God. His will it is that no one getting there shall be deprived of any of the benefits gained by his hardships. For in his lovers he regards sin as a sorrow and a suffering, and, because of his love, not as blameworthy. The reward we will receive will be no small one, but one rather that is great, glorious, and honourable. So shall shame be turned to greater honour and joy.

Our courteous Lord does not want his servants to despair even if they fall frequently and grievously. Our falling does not stop his loving us. Peace and love are always at work in us, but we are not always in peace and love. But he wants us in this way to realize that he is the foundation of the whole of our life in love, and furthermore that he is our eternal protector, and mighty defender against our enemies who are so very fierce and wicked. And, alas, our need is all the greater since we give them every opportunity by our failures.

We must long and love with Jesus, and for love of him shun sin; sin's vileness exceeds all suffering; God's tender love for us in our sin; we need to love our neighbour

40 It is an expression of royal friendship on the part of our courteous Lord that he holds on to us so tenderly when we are in sin, and that, moreover, his touch is so delicate when he shows us our sin by the gentle light of mercy and grace. When we see our self to be so foul, we know that God is angry with us for our sin. In turn we also are

moved by the Holy Spirit to pray contritely, desiring to amend our life to the best of our ability, that we may quench the anger of God and find rest of soul, and an easy conscience. Then we hope that God has forgiven us our sins. And so he has! It is then that our Lord in his courtesy shows himself to the soul, gaily and with cheerful countenance, giving it a friendly welcome as though it had been suffering in prison. 'My beloved,' he says, 'I am glad that you have come to me. In all your trouble I have been with you. Now you can see how I love you. We are made one in blessedness.' So sins are forgiven through merciful grace, and our soul is honourably and joyfully received (just as it will be when it gets to heaven!) whenever it experiences the gracious work of the Holy Spirit, and the virtue of Christ's passion.

By this I know it to be true that all sorts of things are being prepared for us by God's great goodness against that time when we are in peace and in love, and saved in fact. But because it is not possible in this life for us to know this fully, we must endeavour to live with our Lord Jesus in sweet prayer and loving longing. He is always longing to bring us to fullest joy, as was shown earlier when his thirst was revealed.

But if, because of all this spiritual comfort we have been talking of, one were foolish enough to say, 'If this is true, it is a good thing to sin because the reward will be greater', or to hold sin to be less sinful, then beware! Should such a thought come it would be untrue, and would stem from the enemy of the very love that tells of all this comfort. The same blessed love teaches us that we should hate sin for Love's sake alone. I am quite clear about this: the more a soul sees this in the courtesy and love of our Lord God, the more he hates to sin, and the greater is his sense of shame. For if there could be set before us all the pains of hell, purgatory, earth, death, and so on, on the one hand, and sin on the other, we should choose to have all that pain rather than to sin. For sin is so vile and utterly hateful that no pain can compare with it which is not sin. I was shown no harder hell than sin. The soul by its very nature can have no hell but sin.

When we set our will to be loving and humble the effect of mercy and grace is to make everyone beautiful and clean. As mighty and as wise as God is to save men, so great too is his purpose for us. For Christ himself is the foundation of all the laws by which Christians live, and he taught us to prefer good to evil. He himself exemplifies this love, and practises what he preaches. His will is that we should be entirely like him in our continuing love for ourselves and our fellow Christians. His love for us is not broken by our sins; nor does he intend that our love should be broken for ourselves or our fellow Christians. We are to hate sin absolutely, we are to love the soul eternally, just as God loves it. Our hatred of sin will be like God's hatred of it: our love of the soul like God's. This word he has said is continual comfort: 'I keep you securely.'

The fourteenth revelation: we cannot pray for mercy and not have it; God wills us to pray always, even in aridity; such prayer pleases him

41 AFTER this our Lord showed me about prayer. The result of this revelation is that I now see that there are two conditions about prayer. One concerns its rightness, the other our sure trust.

Often enough our trust is not wholehearted, for we are not sure that God hears us. We think it is due to our unworthiness and because we feel absolutely nothing: we are often as barren and dry after our prayers as we were before. This awareness of our foolishness is the cause of our weakness. At least, this has been my own experience.

All this our Lord brought immediately to mind, and in this revelation said, 'I am the foundation of your praying. In the first place my will is that you should pray, and then I make it your will too, and since it is I who make you pray, and you do so pray, how can you not have what you ask for?'

Thus in this first reason, and the three that follow, our good Lord showed me great comfort, as can be gathered from his words. In the first reason, when he says 'and you do so pray', he reveals his great pleasure, and the eternal reward that he gives to us who pray. In the second reason, where he says 'how can you not have?', he is talking of something which is not possible; for it is quite impossible that we should pray for mercy and grace, and not receive it! Everything that our Lord makes us ask for he has ordained for us from before time. So now we can see that it is not our praying that is the cause of God's goodness to us. He showed this to be true in that lovely word, 'I am the foundation.' It is our Lord's will that this truth be known by all his earthly lovers. The more we know it to be true, the more we shall pray, if we are sensible. This is our Lord's meaning.

Prayer is the deliberate act of the soul. It is true, full of grace, and lasting, for it is united with and fixed into the will of our Lord by the inner working of the Holy Spirit. Our Lord himself is the first to receive the prayer – as I see it – and he accepts it gratefully and joyfully. Then he sends it up above, and puts it in the treasury where it will never perish. There it remains continually, before God and his holy ones, ever helping our needs. And when we come to our bliss it shall be given back to us, a contribution to our joy, with his eternal, glorious, gratitude.

Our Lord is greatly cheered by our prayer. He looks for it, and he wants it. By his grace he aims to make us as like himself in heart as we are already in our human nature. This is his blessed will. So he says, 'Pray inwardly, even if you do not enjoy it. It does good, though you feel nothing, see nothing. Yes, even though you think you are doing nothing. For when you are dry, empty, sick, or weak, at such a time is your prayer most pleasing to me though you find little enough to enjoy in it. This is true of all believing prayer.'

Because of the reward and everlasting gratitude he wants us to have, he is eager to see us pray always. God accepts his servant's intention and effort, whatever our feelings. It pleases him that we should work away at our praying and at our Christian living by the help of his grace, and that we consciously direct all our powers to him, until such time as, in all fullness of joy, we have him whom we seek, Jesus. This is the burden of the fifth revelation earlier on, where he says, 'You will have me as your reward.'*

With prayer goes gratitude. Thanksgiving is a real, interior, knowledge. With great reverence and loving fear, it turns us with all our powers to do whatever our good Lord indicates. It brings joy and gratitude within. Sometimes its very abundance gives voice, 'Good Lord, thank you and bless you!' And sometimes when the heart is dry and unfeeling – or it may be because of the enemy's tempting – then reason and grace drive us to cry aloud to our Lord, recalling his blessed passion and great goodness. And the strength of our Lord's word comes to the soul, and fires the heart, and leads it by grace into its real business, enabling it to pray happily and to enjoy our Lord in truth. Thanksgiving is a blessed thing in his sight.

* In fact, these words occur in the fifteenth revelation. But the thought of the present passage is closer to the spirit of the fifth, and though one manuscript corrects 'fifth' to 'fifteenth', Julian's scribe probably did write 'fifth'.

Three matters concerning prayer; how we are to pray; God's goodness makes up our imperfections and weakness when we do what we ought to do

42 OUR Lord God's will is that we should have a real understanding of prayer, and in particular of three things. The first is to know through whom and how our prayer starts. He shows through whom when he says, 'I am the foundation', and he shows how, when by his goodness he says, 'It is my will.' The second is to know how we should best use prayer. The answer is, in fact, that our will should be joyfully subject to the will of the Lord. This is the meaning of 'I make you to will it.' The third is that we should know what is the outcome and purpose of our prayers, namely, that we should be united with our Lord and like him in everything. This is the intention and reason behind this loving lesson. He will help us, and we shall make what he says be true. Bless him!

This is our Lord's intention: that our prayer and our trust alike be large hearted. If we do not trust as much as we pray we do not fully honour our Lord in our prayer; too, we harm and hold ourselves up. The cause, I believe, is due to our not realizing fully that our Lord is the foundation from which our prayer starts. Nor do we realize that our ability to pray is itself given us by his loving grace. For if we did know this, it would mean that we really believed that we should have all we wanted, given by our Lord. I am sure that no one genuinely asks for mercy and grace without mercy and grace having been given him first.

Sometimes it seems to us that we have been praying a long time, and yet we do not see any answer. We should not get despondent because of this. I believe our Lord intends by this either that we should await a more suitable time, or more grace, or a better gift. He wills that we should have a true knowledge of himself that he is all-being: our understanding must be rooted in the knowledge, as strongly, deliberately, and sincerely as we are able to make it. Here we are to stand and stay. By his own gracious light he wants us to understand the following things: (i) the distinction and excellence of our creation, (ii) the price and value of our redemption, and (iii) everything created has been put under us to serve us, and is upheld by him out of love for us. This is his meaning, as if to say, 'See, I have done all this long before your prayers; and now you exist, and pray to me.' He means that we ought to know that the greatest deeds are already done, as Holy Church teaches. Gratefully realizing this we ought to be praying for the deed now in process, which is that he should rule and guide us in this life for his own glory, and bring us to his bliss. It is for this reason that he has done it all. Moreover he intends that just as we see him to be doing it, so we should pray for it as well. It is not enough just to do one without the other. For if we pray, not realizing that he is already at work, it makes us despondent and sceptical – which is not honouring to him. And if we see him at work yet do not pray, we do less than we ought. May that not happen – and may he not see it so! But to see that he is doing it, and to pray for it at the same time – that honours him, and benefits us. Everything our Lord has ordained to do he wishes us to pray for either specifically or generally. His consequent happiness and joy, and our thanks and glory, pass our power to understand.

For prayer is the means whereby we rightly understand the fullness of joy that is coming to us: it is true longing, and sure trust too. Lack of the happiness which is our natural lot makes us long for it. Real understanding, love, and the recollection of our Saviour enables us to trust. Our Lord sees us constantly at work at these two things. It is no more than our duty, and no less than his goodness would assign to us. It is up to us to do our part with diligence, yet when we have done it, it will seem to us that we have done nothing ... and rightly so. But if we do what we can, and truly ask mercy and grace, all that we lack we shall find in him. 'I am the foundation of your praying' means this. So in this blessed word, together with the revelation, I saw the complete victory over all our weakness and our doubting fear.

What prayer effects when in line with God's will; God's goodness delights in his deeds done through us, as though he were indebted to us; all things work sweetly

43 PRAYER unites the soul to God. However like God the soul may be in essence and nature (once it has been restored by grace), it is often unlike him in fact because of man's sin. Then it is that prayer proclaims that the soul should will what God wills; and it strengthens the conscience and enables a man to obtain grace. God teaches us to pray thus, and to trust firmly that we shall have what we ask. For he looks at us in love, and would have us share in his good work. So he moves us to pray for what it is he wants to do. For such prayer and good will – and it is his gift – he rewards us eternally. And the word 'and you do so pray' shows all this. In it God takes as great pleasure and delight as if he were indebted to us for all the good we do. And yet it is he who actually does it! Because we pray earnestly that he should do whatever he wills, it is as though he said, 'What can please me more than to have you pray fervently, wisely, and earnestly to do what I am going to do?' So does the soul by prayer conform to God.

But when our Lord in his courtesy and grace shows himself to our soul we have what we desire. Then we care no longer about praying for any thing, for our whole strength and aim is set on beholding. This is prayer, high and ineffable, in my eyes. The whole reason why we pray is summed up in the sight and vision of him to whom we pray. Wondering, enjoying, worshipping, fearing ... and all with such sweetness and delight that during that time we can only pray in such ways as he leads us. Well do I know that the more the soul sees God, the more by his grace does it want him.

But when we do not see him thus, we feel the more need to pray to Jesus because of our basic failure and incapacity. For when the soul is tossed and troubled and alone in its unrest, it is time to pray so as to make itself sensitive and submissive to God. Of course prayer cannot in any way make God sensitive to the soul: for this is what, in his love, he always is. And I realized, moreover, that when we know we have got to pray, then our good Lord follows this up, helping our desire. And when by his special grace we see him clearly, there is need of nothing further. We have to follow him, drawn by his love into himself. For I saw and knew that his marvellous and utter goodness brings our powers up to their full strength. At the same time I saw that he is at work unceasingly in every conceivable thing, and that it is all done so well, so wisely, and so powerfully that it is far greater than anything we can imagine, guess, or think. Then we can do no more than gaze in delight with a tremendous desire to be wholly united to him, to live where he lives, to enjoy his love, and to delight in his goodness. It is then that we, through our humble, persevering prayer, and the help of his grace, come to him now, in this present life. There will be many secret touches that we shall feel and see, sweet and spiritual, and adapted to our ability to receive them. This is achieved by the grace of the Holy Spirit, both now and until the time that, still longing and loving, we die. On that day we shall come to our Lord knowing our self clearly, possessing God completely. Eternally 'hid in God' we shall see him truly and feel him fully, hear him spiritually, smell him delightfully, and taste him sweetly! We shall see God face to face, simply and fully. The creature, made by God, shall see and eternally gaze upon him, his Maker. 'No man may see God and live' in this mortal life. But when by special grace he reveals himself here, he strengthens the creature above its natural capacity, and he adjusts the revelation as he wills, and as best serves the occasion.

Attributes of the Trinity; created man has the same attributes when he does what he was made for; he sees, gazes, and marvels at God, and sees himself to be nothing

44 IN all these revelations God frequently showed that man was always doing God's will, and ever expressing his worth. What this work is in fact was shown in the first revelation, in that wonderful example of the action of truth and wisdom in the soul of our blessed Lady St Mary. How I saw this happen I am hoping to show, by the grace of God.

Truth sees God: wisdom gazes on God. And these two produce a third, a holy, wondering delight in God, which is love. Where there is indeed truth and wisdom, there too is love, springing from them both. And all of God's making: for he is eternal sovereign truth, eternal sovereign wisdom, eternal sovereign love, uncreated. Man's soul is God's creation, and possesses similar properties (only they are created) and it always does what it was created for: it sees God, it gazes on God, and it loves God. And God rejoices in his creature; and his creature in God, eternally marvelling. And in this wonder he sees his God, his Lord, his Maker, so high and great and good that in comparison the creature seems to himself to be nothing. Yet the splendour and clarity of truth enable him to see and to know that he has been made for love; and in that love God everlastingly keeps him.

The strong, deep judgement of God, and the changeable judgement of men

45 GOD judges us according to our essential nature, which is for ever kept whole, safe, and sound in him. And his judgement is according to his righteousness. But man judges according to his changeable feelings, which are now this, now that, and which vary with his particular mood, and display themselves outwardly. Man's judgement is confused, inconsistent: sometimes it is good and tolerant, sometimes it is harsh and difficult. When it is good and tolerant it is part of God's righteousness, and when it is harsh and difficult our good Lord Jesus reforms it by the action of that mercy and grace which are the result of his blessed passion. In this way he brings it into line with his righteousness. Yet though these two judgements are hereby reconciled and united, each one will ever be known separately in heaven.

The first judgement is according to his righteousness, which was shown when his supreme and eternal life took on the substance of our nature. This gracious judgement I saw throughout the whole of that lovely revelation in which he attributed no blame to us. Yet however delightful all this might be, the sight of this in itself did not bring complete satisfaction. I was aware of the judgement of Holy Church which I had seen earlier, and which was constantly before my eyes. Because of this latter judgement I knew that I must recognize myself as a sinner, and by the same token I realized that sinners sometimes deserve God's blame and wrath. But since I could find neither of these in God, my longing to know was more than can or should be told. For the higher judgement God himself showed me, and I had necessarily to accept it: the lesser judgement had been taught me previously by Holy Church, and for that reason I could not dismiss it.

This then was what I was wanting: to see, in God, how the judgement taught by Holy Church can be true in his sight, and how I might indubitably know it: in other words to reconcile the two judgements, so that God's honour was preserved, and I could see it to be right.

The only solution I found was in a wonderful illustration of a lord and his servant, which I will recount later. Even that was not wholly clear. Yet I still want to know, and shall do till I die, what by grace these two judgements signify for me. For all heavenly things, and all earthly things – which belong to heaven – are embraced by these two judgements. And the more we can understand them, under the guidance of the Holy Spirit, the greater will be our insight into our own failings. And the more too, will we long, both naturally and by grace, to be filled with eternal joy and happiness. We have been made for this, and our natural being is even now happy in God, as it always has been, and indeed ever shall be.

We can only know ourselves in this life through faith and grace; we must know how sinful we are as sinners; God is never angry; he is nearest of all to the soul, and preserves it

46 OUR fleeting life here, with its physical senses, does not know what our real self is, but in that Day we will see it truly and clearly, and know our Lord in fullness of joy. The nearer we are to happiness, the more we necessarily long for it, both naturally and by grace. We can have some knowledge of our self in this life through the regular help and assistance of our higher nature. And this knowledge we can strengthen and develop, helped on by merciful grace. But we shall never wholly know our self until the very last moment, when this passing life with its pain and woe shall

come to its end. Therefore it is wholly fitting, both in nature and grace, that we should long with all our might to know our self in the fullness of eternal joy.

Throughout all this, from beginning to end, I was aware of two things. One was of unending, continuing love, with the assurance and the blessedness of salvation – this was the whole point of the revelation. The other was the common teaching of Holy Church, in which I had been instructed and grounded of old, and which I make use of every day and which I understand. I did not lose this latter awareness, for I was not for a moment drawn away from it by this revelation. Rather my experience taught me to love and appreciate it, so that I might, by the help of our Lord's grace, increase and rise to even greater heavenly knowledge and love.

So throughout the vision I thought I was being obliged to recognize that we are sinners, who commit many evil things that ought not to be done, and who omit many good deeds that ought to be done. We deserve to suffer pain and God's anger! Yet in spite of all this I saw plainly that our Lord was never angry – nor would be. For he is God – goodness, life, truth, love, peace, The integrity of his love will not permit him to be angry. I saw that it is contrary to the nature of his power, his wisdom, and goodness to be angry. God is the goodness that may not be angry, for he is nothing but goodness. Our soul is united to him who is unchangeable goodness, and between him and our soul there is need neither for anger nor forgiveness in his sight. For the soul is completely united to God by his own goodness, and nothing whatever can come between God and the soul.

To this conclusion was the soul lovingly led and strongly drawn in every revelation. That is how our good Lord showed it, and that is how it is in fact through his great goodness. And he wants us to want to know it: as far as is possible for his creation to learn it. Everything that my simple soul understood, God wanted to be revealed and made known. It is the secret things that he hides with power and wisdom for love's sake. I saw in the same revelation that there is much secret that is hidden, which will never be known until that time when God in his goodness had made us worthy to see it. I am well content to accept our Lord's will in this wonderful matter. And I surrender to my mother, Holy Church, as a simple child ought.

We must wonder in reverence, suffer in humility, and always rejoice in God; sin is the cause of the blindness which prevents us from seeing God

47 OUR soul has a twofold duty: to wonder in all reverence, and to suffer in all humility, even while we always rejoice in God. He wants us to know how soon we shall see clearly in himself all that we are longing for.

Notwithstanding all this I was still much puzzled. What is the mercy and forgiveness of God? My earlier teaching had been that the mercy of God was shown in the forgiving of his anger after we had sinned. For I thought that for a soul whose intention and desire is to love God, his wrath was more difficult to bear than any other sort of pain, and therefore I took it that its forgiveness would be one of the chief things about his mercy. But for all my great desire to understand this, in the various revelations I was unable to see anything of the kind.

But as God gives me grace I will tell something of what I did understand and see of the work of mercy. I understood this: man is fickle in this life, and by his frailty and ignorance falls into sin. He is essentially weak and foolish, and his will can be overborne. In his lifetime he experiences storms, sorrows, and grief; and the reason is that he is blind: he does not see God. If he saw God continually he would have no mischievous feelings, or any sort of urge or desire that led to sin. So it appeared to me at the time, and I thought that this insight I experienced was vivid and full and real compared with my normal reactions. Even so it seemed mean and petty alongside the great desire of the soul for God.

I felt that there were five sorts of activity in me, and they were these: rejoicing, mourning, longing, fearing, and confident hoping. Rejoicing certainly, for God gave me the understanding and knowledge that it was himself that I saw; mourning, too, over my failings; longing, that I might ever see him more and more, though with the knowledge that we shall never fully rest until we see him really and clearly in heaven; yet fearing, for I was afraid all the time that my vision would fail and I should be left to myself; and all with a confident hope in that eternal love, by which I saw I should be kept by his mercy and brought to his blessedness.

The joy in this sight, together with the confident hope of his merciful keeping, gave me such comfort that the mourning and fearing were not too painful. Yet at the same time I realized, in this revelation of God, that this way of seeing him would not necessarily persist through life – for the sake of his own honour, and for our own growth in everlasting joy. This is the reason why we often lose sight of him. Then we turn back on to our self, there to find no sense of being right, but rather the perversity of that self, which has sprung from the old root of our first sin, and all the other sins that have followed on with our consent. And so we are tossed and tormented with the feeling of sin and pain in all those various and familiar ways, both spiritual and physical.

*The attributes of mercy and grace; we shall rejoice over our patient
enduring of trouble*

48 BUT our good Lord, the Holy Spirit, who is everlasting life and who securely dwells in our soul, keeps
us, and by his grace produces a real peace, Godlike and docile.
In this merciful fashion our Lord is always leading us amidst
the changes and chances of this mortal life.

I saw no anger other than human – and that God forgives.
This anger is nothing else but perverse opposition to peace
and love; it comes from the failure of our own strength, or
wisdom, or goodness. This is a failure of ourselves, not of God.
By our wretched sinning we are in constant opposition to
peace and love. Our Lord often expressed that in his loving
looks of compassion and pity. The basis of mercy is love, and
it is the business of mercy to keep us in love. This was shown
me in such a way that I could not possibly dissociate mercy
from love. I speak, of course, of the way I see it. For mercy
works in love, sweetly, generously, compassionately. Mercy
works in us, keeping us, and turning everything to good
account. Mercy, through love, allows us to fail, at least in
part, and the measure of our failure is the measure of our fall,
and because we fall we die. For inevitably we die when our
sight or awareness of him who is our life fails. Our failure is
dreadful, our fall shameful, our dying lamentable, yet never
once does that dear eye of love and pity cease to regard us, nor
his mercy fail.

For I saw what mercy and grace were like. Both function
differently, but in the same love. Mercy is compassionate with
the tender love of motherhood. Grace on the other hand is
most honourable, the quality of regal lordship, yet equally
loving. Mercy works to sustain, to suffer, to vitalize, to heal;
and all in the tenderest love. Grace works to uplift, to reward,

and ever to surpass all we desire or deserve. In this way it makes known and displays the supreme, many-sided generosity of God, our Lord and King, and his exquisite courtesy. All this through his abounding love! For grace can turn our dreadful failure into abundant and eternal comfort, our shameful fall into honourable recovery, our lamentable dying into holy and blessed life.

I saw clearly that just as our perversity results in pain, shame and sorrow here below, so in heaven grace produces consolation, honour, and blessedness. And so superlatively, that when we come to receive the reward that grace has won for us, we shall thank and bless God, rejoicing evermore that once we suffered. And the nature of this blessed love is such that we shall know in God what we should never have known, had we not suffered previously. And when I saw this, I had to admit that God's mercy and forgiveness does mitigate and make void our anger.

Our life is grounded in love; we cannot live otherwise; God is never angry; despite our anger and sin he mercifully preserves us, and brings peace; he rewards our troubles

49 A CONSTANTLY recurring feature of all the revelations which filled my soul with wonder as I diligently observed it, was that our Lord God, as far as he himself is concerned, does not have to forgive, because it is impossible for him to be angry! It was shown that the whole of life is grounded and rooted in love, and that without love we cannot live. So to the soul, privileged by grace to see deeply into the marvellous goodness of God, and to see that we are eternally united to him in love, it is absolutely impossible that God should be angry. Anger and friendship are mutually opposed.

And he who mitigates and eliminates our anger and makes us humble and gentle, must surely need himself to be loving, humble, and gentle. And that is the opposite of anger.

It is quite clear that where our Lord is, peace reigns and anger has no place. I could see no sort of anger in God, however long I looked. Indeed, if God were to be angry but for a moment we could not live, endure, or be! Just as we owe our existence to God's everlasting might, wisdom, and goodness, so by these same qualities are we kept in being. And though we wretches know from our own experience the meaning of discord and tension, we are still surrounded in every conceivable way by God's gentleness and humility, his kindness and graciousness. I saw quite clearly that our eternal friendship, our continuing life and existence is in God.

The same eternal goodness that keeps us from perishing when we sin keeps on giving a peace which offsets our own anger and wrong-headed falling. It makes us realize with a genuine dread what is our real need; it urges us strongly to seek God and his forgiveness; by God's grace it makes us want salvation. We cannot be safe and happy until we know real love and peace: that is what salvation is. Even if we, through our own anger and wrong-headedness, do have to go through hardship and discomfort and trouble, which are the outcome of our blind weakness, we are still kept safe and sound by the mercy of God, so that we do not perish. But there will be no joyful salvation or eternal happiness until we are completely at peace and in love. In other words, until we are wholly content with God, his actions, and decisions; until we are in love and at peace with ourselves, our fellow Christians, and with all that God loves. Love is like that. And it is God's goodness that effects this in us.

Thus I saw God to be our true peace, who keeps us safe when we are anything but peaceful, and who always works to bring us to everlasting peace. So when, by the action of his merciful grace, we are made humble and gentle, we are indeed safe. The soul, when it is really at peace with itself, is at once united to God. No anger is found in God. And I realized that when we are in complete and loving peace there is no opposition to God, or any sort of resistance such as we put up now. Indeed the goodness of our Lord turns all this to our profit. The troubles and sorrows, caused by our perversity, the Lord Jesus takes, and lifts up to heaven where they are transformed to things of delight and pleasure greater than heart can think or tongue can tell. And when we get there ourselves we shall find them waiting for us changed into things of beautiful and eternal worth. God is our sure foundation. And he is going to be our fullest bliss, and even as he is himself in heaven so will he make us – unchangeable!

The elect soul has never been dead in the sight of God; Julian's wonder at this, and the three reasons why she dared ask God for further enlightenment

50 IN this mortal life we can only travel by the way of God's mercy and forgiveness, and they always lead us to his grace. Because of the trouble and distress that we ourselves fall into, human judgement must often regard us as spiritually dead, but in God's sight the soul to be saved never was dead, and never will be.

Yet here I had to wonder, and to puzzle out in my soul this great question, 'Good Lord, I can see you are real truth, and I know too that we sin, indeed grievously every day, and are most blameworthy. I can never hide from you the truth about myself, and yet I never see you blame us. How is this?' The normal teaching of Holy Church and, indeed, my own experience, told me of the blame of sin which has been hanging over us, from the time of Adam until we reach heaven. It was the more surprising that I should see the Lord God regard us with no more blame than if we had been as pure and holy as his angels in heaven. Between these two opposites my mind was extremely perplexed. I could not see how to reconcile them, nor could I relax for fear that I might lose sight of his blessed presence and be left ignorant how he could regard us still in all our sin. There were two alternatives: either I must acknowledge that with God there is no such thing as sin, or else I must discover how he does in fact regard it, so that I could see it in the same light. That goes for our blame too. My longing for him persisted, and the vision of him continued, yet I could not settle because of this aweful perplexity. I thought, 'If I assume that we are not sinners, or blameworthy, surely such thinking must be at fault, and I must be ignorant of the truth. On the other hand, if we are indeed sinners and culpable . . . Good Lord, how is it that I cannot see this truth in you, my God and Creator, in whom I long to see all truths?'

Three things force me to ask such a question: (i) Sin is such a paltry thing. If it had been a great thing I should be terrified. (ii) Sin is so widespread. Had it been peculiar to myself, again I should be terrified. (iii) If I am to live here with a knowledge of good and evil it is essential for me to be able to distinguish one from the other, so that I love goodness and hate evil, as Holy Church teaches. So I cried in my spirit, earnestly asking God for help, 'Lord Jesus, King of bliss, how can I find the answer? Who will teach me and tell me what I need to know, if I cannot see it now in yourself?'

*God's answer to this doubt of hers, given in the wonderful illustra-
tion of a lord and his servant; God wills that we should wait for
him, for it was nearly twenty years before Julian understood
this example; Christ sits at the Father's right hand; how this
is to be understood*

51 AND then, in his courtesy, our Lord answered me, by
giving me the mysterious and wonderful illustration of
the lord who had a servant. And he helped me to understand
the significance of each of them. In the lord and in the servant
alike I saw a twofold truth expressed; I saw it first in my spirit
in physical outline, and then it was shown more spiritually
without any such outline.

The first time I saw physically before me two people, a lord
and his servant. And God showed me its spiritual meaning.
The lord is sitting down quietly, relaxed and peaceful: the
servant is standing by his lord, humble and ready to do his
bidding. And then I saw the lord look at his servant with rare
love and tenderness, and quietly send him to a certain place to
fulfil his purpose. Not only does that servant go, but he starts
off at once, running with all speed, in his love to do what his
master wanted. And without warning he falls headlong into a
deep ditch, and injures himself very badly. And though he
groans and moans and cries and struggles he is quite unable to
get up or help himself in any way. To crown all, he could get
no relief of any sort: he could not even turn his head to look
at the lord who loved him, and who was so close to him. The
sight of him would have been of real comfort, but he was
temporarily so weak and bemused that he gave vent to his
feelings, as he suffered his pains.

His pain was sevenfold. First of all there was the severe
bruising which resulted from his fall, and was hurting very

much; then there was the sheer weight of his body; thirdly there was the consequent weakness following these two factors; fourthly his mind was shocked, and he could not see the reason for it all – so that he almost forgot the love that had spurred him on; and there was the fifth and further fact that he could not get up; moreover, in the sixth place – and this I found quite extraordinary – he was quite alone: wherever I looked, high and low, far and near, I could see none to help him; and lastly there was the hard rough surface on to which he had fallen.

I was greatly surprised to see with what humility this servant endured such suffering and I sought most carefully to find some fault in him, and to know if his lord regarded him as blameworthy. And, in truth, I could see neither. Basically it was his own good will and great longing that had caused his fall; he was still as loyal and goodhearted as when he stood before his lord, ready to do his bidding. And it is thus that his master always sees him. But now the sense in which he regarded him was twofold. There was the obvious primary one, humble, gentle, compassionate, and pitying – this was the first; and there was the second one, inner and more spiritual, which when it was showed me helped me to enter into the mind of his lord. He was delighting in the thought of the well-earned rest and great honour which in his abundant generosity he was planning to give his servant. This was all part of the inner significance, and it led me back to think of the first, not however to the exclusion of the second. It was as though his thoughtful lord were saying, 'Here is my servant whom I love. What hurt and discomfort he has known in my service – and all out of love for me, due to his own generous nature! Surely it would be right to reward him for all this terror and fright, this hurt, injury, and grief? Ought I not to give him something that will more than compensate him, and indeed, be even more worth having than his own previous health?

If I did otherwise I should be showing no gratitude at all!'

I began to see now an inner, spiritual significance attaching to the lord's words. The natural consequence of his great goodness and worth was that his much beloved servant should be truly and gladly rewarded beyond anything he could have had had he not fallen. Yes, indeed, further; his fall and subsequent suffering were to be transformed into great and superlative honour and everlasting joy.

At this point the picture vanished, and our Lord then enlightened me with regard to this revelation. Yet for all his guidance, my puzzlement over the illustration never left me. I thought that it had been given as an answer to my request, yet at the same time I was unable to find a wholly satisfying meaning in it. The *servant* stood for Adam, as I shall be saying, but on the other hand there were many characteristics that could not possibly be ascribed to him. So there I had to leave it, a large part unknown. The full meaning of this marvellous illustration was not at that time shown me. Yet hidden deep down in this great picture are three particular attributes of the revelation. Indeed I now began to understand that every revelation was full of deep secrets. So I will now speak of those three qualities which bring some relief to my mind.

The first quality is the literal meaning of the words as I then received them; the second is the inner significance that I have discovered since; the third is the whole revelation itself, which, from beginning to end – covering the contents of this book – God in his goodness brings to mind, often and freely. As I understand it these three are so much one that I cannot – indeed, may not – separate them. And by these three-and-one I have been taught to believe and trust that our Lord God, through the same goodness by which he first revealed it, and for the same reason, will later in similar fashion make it known to us when he so wills.

After twenty years (all but three months) from the time of the revelation I received inner enlightenment, as I am going to tell: 'It is for you to consider all the details and circumstances shown in the illustration; even if you think they are vague and unimportant.' I assented wholeheartedly and eagerly, and began to give close attention to all the points and details that had been shown at that time, as far as my ability to understand would allow. I began with the lord and the servant as I saw them: how and where the lord sat; the colour and cut of his clothes; his appearance, and his innate nobility and goodness; and how and where the servant stood, what his clothes were like, and their colour and style; his outward bearing and his inner goodness and loyalty.

The *lord* who was sitting in solemn state, quietly and peacefully, I took to be God. The *servant* who stood before his lord I understood to be Adam. There was shown at that time just one man and his fall; to make us understand that God sees Everyman and his fall. In the sight of God everyman is one man, and one man is everyman. This man's strength was injured, and he was much weakened. His senses too were confused, for he turned away from looking at his lord. However his will was still sound in God's sight, for I saw that our Lord commended and approved his will. But he was prevented from seeing this about his will, and therefore was in great sorrow and distress. He could not see clearly his loving lord, so gentle and kind towards him, nor could he see how he really stood in the eyes of that same loving master. Well do I know that when we are really certain about these two things, even here we can savour something of their peace and rest, while in heaven by God's bountiful grace we shall enjoy them in their fullness.

At this time I began to learn how it is that God can still behold us in our sin. I went on to see that it is only pain that blames and punishes, but that our gracious Lord comforts and sympathizes, for he is ever kindly disposed towards our soul, and, loving us, longs to bring us to his bliss. It was a simple sort of place where the lord was sitting. It was the earth, bare, deserted, lonely, wild. His clothes were full and flowing and seemly. Their colour was the blue of the sky, restrained but beautiful; his countenance full of pity; his face was a light tan in colour and he had regular features; his eyes were dark, beautiful, and true, filled with loving compassion. There was deep and generous insight, full of eternity and heaven. And I thought that the love with which he ceaselessly regarded his servant, especially when he fell, would melt our own hearts with love and break them for very joy. This lovely gaze displayed a wonderful and fitting blend of compassion and pity, of joy and blessedness. The latter surpassed the former as the heaven does the earth. Pity was earthly, blessedness heavenly. The compassion and pity was that of the Father when his most loved creation, Adam, fell; the joy and blessedness was in his own beloved Son who is equal with the Father. The merciful gaze of his loving eyes ranged the whole earth, and went down with Adam into hell; his continuing pity kept Adam from eternal death. Mercy and pity dwell thus with mankind until at last we come to heaven. But man in this life is blind and cannot see God, our Father, as he is. And whenever he wills of his goodness to show himself to man, he shows himself in great simplicity, as man. All the same I saw quite clearly that we ought to know and believe that the Father is not man.

But his sitting on the bare, deserted, *earth* means this: he made man's soul to be his own city and his home. Of all his works this is the one that most pleases him. When man fell into sorrow and pain, he became unfit to serve in that noble office, yet our kind Father would prepare no other place for himself, but would sit upon the earth, waiting for mankind (itself compounded of earth), until such time as, by his grace, his beloved son had restored his city to its noble beauty through his tremendous effort.

The *blue* of his clothes symbolized his constancy; the tone of that distinguished *face* and the *dark eyes* combined to show his serious intent; the *ample nature* of his clothes, beautiful and radiant, suggested that he had within himself all heaven, all joy, all happiness. This first struck me when I was speaking of being 'helped to enter into the mind of his lord', for I saw him rejoicing at the honour to which he intended to restore his servant.

I still had cause to marvel as I beheld this lord and his servant. I saw the lord sitting in solemn state, and his servant standing reverently before him. In the servant there is a twofold significance, outward and inner. Outwardly he was dressed simply, like a man ready for work, and he stood very near his lord, not straight in front of him, but slightly to the side, on the left. He was wearing a single white coat, old and worn, stained with sweat, tight and short, coming just below the knee, threadbare, almost worn out, ready to fall apart any moment. I was very surprised at this for I thought it was most unsuitable garb for a much loved servant to wear in the presence of his honoured lord. But I realized that there was in him a fundamental love, a love for his lord equal to that of his lord for him. The servant was wise enough to know that there was but one thing to do to be worthy of his master. And for love, regardless of himself or the consequences, the servant at once started off, and ran at the bidding of his lord, to do whatever was his will, and that brought him honour. Outwardly he looked as if he had been working hard for a long time, but to my inner understanding he seemed to be a beginner, new to hard work, a servant who had never been sent out before.

There was an earthly treasure which the lord loved. I wondered what it might be, and the answer came to mind, 'It is a repast, lovely and pleasing to the lord.' For though the lord was sitting down as any man would, I could see no food or drink to give him. This was surprising in itself. Still more surprising was the fact that this great man had no servant but one, and him he sent off. I went on looking, wondering what sort of work the servant had to do. Then I understood: he was off to do work that was the hardest and most exhausting possible. He was to be a gardener, digging and banking, toiling and sweating, turning and trenching the ground, watering the plants the while. And by keeping at this work he would make sweet streams to flow, fine abundant fruits to grow; he would bring them to his lord, and serve them to his taste. And he would not return till he had prepared the meal just as he knew his master would like it. Then he would take it, and the appropriate refreshment, bearing them with due ceremony to his lord. And all the time the lord would be sitting where he had left him, waiting for the servant he had sent out.

I still puzzled where the servant came from. I saw that in the lord there was everlasting life and every goodness, except the treasure that was in the earth. And that treasure too had its being in the wonderful depth of his eternal love. But its worth to him depended on the servant's careful preparation of it, and his setting it before him, personally. All around the master was nothing but wilderness. I did not understand all that this example meant, so I still puzzled where the servant came from.

In the *servant* is represented the second Person of the Trinity; and in the *servant* again Adam, or in other words, Everyman. When I speak of the *Son* I am thinking of the Godhead which is equal to the Father's, and when I say the *servant* I have Christ's human nature in mind. He is the true Adam. The *nearness* of the servant has to do with the Son, and the *standing on the left side* refers to Adam. The *lord* is God the Father, the *servant* is the Son, Jesus Christ; the Holy Spirit is the *love* that is common to them both.

When Adam *fell*, God's Son fell. Because of the true unity

which had been decreed in heaven, God's Son could not be dissociated from Adam. By *Adam* I always understand *Everyman*. Adam fell from life to death, first into the depths of this wretched world, and then into hell. God's Son fell, with Adam, but into the depth of the Virgin's womb – herself the fairest daughter of Adam – with the intent of excusing Adam from blame both in heaven and on earth. And with a mighty arm he brought him out of hell. By the servant's *wisdom* and *goodness* the Son is understood. The *poor clothes* of the workman standing near the left is a reference to human nature, and Adam, and all the subsequent mischief and weakness. In all this the good Lord showed his own Son and Adam as one man. Our virtue and goodness are due to Jesus Christ, our weakness and blindness to Adam; and both were shown in the one servant. In this way we can see how our good Lord Jesus has taken upon himself all our blame, and that, as a result, our Father cannot and will not blame us more than his own dear Son, Jesus Christ. So the servant, before he came to this world *stood before* his Father, ready for his will and against the time he should be *sent* to do that most worthy deed by which mankind was brought back to heaven. And this, notwithstanding he is God, equal with his Father in respect of his Godhead. In his future purpose he was to be Man, to save man by fulfilling his Father's will. So he stood before his Father as a servant, deliberately, making himself responsible for us.

He started off with all eagerness at his Father's will, and at once he fell low, into the Virgin's womb, regardless of himself or his hard lot. The *white coat* is his flesh; its being *single* the fact that there is nothing separating Godhead and human nature; its *tight fit* is poverty, its *age* is Adam's wearing of it, its *sweat stains* Adam's toil, its *shortness*, the work the servant did. And I saw the Son saying in effect, 'Dear Father, I stand before you in Adam's stead, ready to start off and run. My will is to go to earth and bring you honour, whenever you wish to send me. How long am I to desire this?' The Son knew with absolute certainty when the Father's will would be, and how long he would have to wait for it. But this he knew in respect of his Godhead, for he is the wisdom of the Father. His query however was made in virtue of his manhood. For all the humanity that will be saved by his blessed incarnation and passion is included in Christ's humanity; for he is the head, and we are his members. To us members are unknown the day and time when all these temporary griefs and sorrows will be done away, and joy and blessedness be eternally achieved. To know this hour the whole company of heaven is longing! The way to heaven for those of us who are not yet members is by longing and desire. And we saw this longing and desire in the servant's *standing* before his lord, or rather in the Son's standing before his Father in Adam's coat. The heartfelt desire that mankind has to be saved appeared in Jesus. Jesus is everyone that will be saved, and everyone that will be saved is Jesus – all through the charity of God; and through virtue, obedience, humility and patience, on our part.

Moreover, in this wonderful example there is teaching for me which is like beginning the ABC. It gives me some inkling of our Lord's meaning. The secrets of this whole revelation are hidden in it – though of course each individual revelation is full of secrets. That the Father *sits* is a sign of his Godhead: it shows rest and peace, for in the Godhead there can be no activity. That he showed himself *lord* is a sign of his authority over our humanity. The servant's *standing* means however that he is active, and the *left side* shows he was not worthy to stand on an equal footing with the lord. The *starting* is a reference to his Godhead, the *running* to his humanity, for the Godhead started from the Father to enter the Virgin's womb, falling, as it were, to take our human nature upon himself. Thereby he accepted great hurt, the hurt which was our flesh, in which from the first he experienced mortal pain. By his *standing reverently* before his lord but not in front of him, we are to understand that his garb was not suitable for the presence of his lord; indeed he could not stand in front of him all the while he was a labourer. Nor could he sit or rest peacefully until he had properly won that peace by his own hard work. The *left side* means that the Father deliberately allowed his own son to suffer in his human nature Everyman's pain, without sparing him. By his *coat ready to fall apart* is understood the assault, the flogging, the thorns, the nails, the pulling and pushing, the tearing of his tender flesh. I had already seen this in part at least, when I saw how his flesh had been torn from the skull and had hung in pieces. Then the bleeding had stopped, and it began to dry up, and adhered again to the bone. The *agony* and *struggling*, *groaning* and *moaning* suggest that he could never rise up again in all his power from the moment of his *fall* into the Virgin's womb until his body had been slain and he had yielded his soul (and with it all humanity) into his Father's hands.

From now on he began to show his power. He went down to hell, and there he raised up from the lowest depths that great mass which was his by right, united to him in high heaven. His body lay in the grave until Easter Day. Thereafter it never lay again. For there was rightly ended all the agony and struggling, the moaning and groaning. And our filthy, dying flesh which the Son of God took upon himself, like Adam's old *coat*, *tight*, *threadbare*, and too *short*, the Saviour transformed into something beautiful, fresh, bright and splendid, eternally spotless, *full and flowing*, fairer and richer than even the clothing I had seen on the Father. His clothing was blue, but Christ's was of a harmony and beauty the like and wonder of which I just cannot describe. It could not be more magnificent. Now the lord sits, not on an earthly desert, but on his throne in heaven, as he should. Now the Son stands, no longer a servant before the lord, bowed, shabby, and half-clad, but straight before him as his Father, clothed in rich and blessed amplitude, crowned with priceless splendour. We are his crown, the crown which is the Father's joy, the Son's honour, the Holy Spirit's pleasure, the endless, blessed wonder of all heaven. Now sits the Son, the labourer no longer standing on the Father's left, but sitting at the Father's right, in eternal peace and rest. (We do not mean, of course, that the Son sits literally on the right hand, side by side as people sit here! As I see it there is nothing of this sort in the Holy Trinity. 'To sit at the Father's right hand' means that he enjoys the highest dignity with the Father.) Now is the Bridegroom, God's Son, resting with his beloved wife, the beautiful Virgin, eternally joyful. Now sits the Son, true God and true man, at rest and in peace in his own *city*, that city prepared for him in the eternal purpose of the Father. And the Father in the Son, and the Holy Spirit in the Father and in the Son.

God rejoices to be our Father, Brother, Husband; the life of the elect on earth is a mixture of good and bad; how we can shun sin

52 In this way I saw that God was rejoicing to be our Father; rejoicing too to be our Mother; and rejoicing yet again to be our true Husband, with our soul his beloved wife. And Christ rejoices to be our Brother, and our Saviour too. These five great joys I believe he intends us to enjoy too – praising, thanking, loving, blessing him for ever.

In this life there is within us who are to be saved a surprising mixture of good and bad. We have our risen Lord; we have the wretchedness and mischief done by Adam's fall and death. Kept secure by Christ we are assured, by his touch of grace, of salvation; broken by Adam's fall, and in many ways by our own sins and sorrows, we are so darkened and blinded that we can hardly find any comfort. But in our heart we abide in God, and confidently trust to his mercy and grace – and this is his working in us. And of his goodness he opens the eye of our understanding so that we can *see*; sometimes it is less, sometimes more, according to our God-given ability to receive it. Now we are uplifted by the one; now we are allowed to fall into the other. And this fluctuating is so baffling that we are hard put to know where we stand, whether we are thinking of ourselves or of our fellow believers. It certainly is a marvellous mix up! But the one thing that matters is that we always say 'Yes' to God whenever we experience him, and really do will to be with him, with all our heart and soul and strength. It is then that we hate and despise our evil inclinations, and all else that might make us sin, physically or spiritually. Yet, when this sweetness vanishes, we fall back into our blind state, and so into all sorts of distress and trouble. At such a time this is our strength – we know by faith that, through the virtue of Christ our guardian, we never really accept this situation; but, protesting against it, we hang on and pray through all this trouble and grief, until such time as once again God will reveal himself to us.

This fluctuating persists through life. But it is the will of God that we should trust that he is always with us. He is with us in three ways: he is with us in heaven, as true man, in his own Person raising us with him – that was the significance of the revelation of the spiritual thirst; he is with us on earth leading us – that was shown in the third revelation when I saw the whole Godhead concentrated into a single point; and he is with us in our soul, eternally indwelling, guiding, and keeping us – and that was brought out in the sixteenth revelation as I shall be going on to say.

For example, in the *servant* was shown the harm and the blindness caused by Adam's fall, and again in the *servant* was shown the wisdom and goodness of God's Son. And in the *lord* was shown his compassion and pity for Adam's distress, and in the *lord* again was shown the exalted nobility and eternal honour to which humanity has attained by virtue of the passion and death of his beloved Son. For this reason he rejoices tremendously over his *falling* into the Virgin's womb, because of man's subsequent exaltation and utter happiness, beyond anything we should have known if he had not fallen. I was led by God to understand this surpassing nobility at the very moment I saw the servant fall.

The result is that we now have both matter for mourning – for our sin is the cause of Christ's sufferings – and matter for lasting joy – for his unending love made him suffer. So the creature that sees and experiences the gracious working of love hates nothing but sin, for, as I see it, love and hate are the most difficult and irreconcilable opposites of all. Yet at the same time I recognized that our Lord's meaning was that it was not expected that we should be able to keep ourselves as wholly free and clean of sin as we shall be later in heaven. But by grace we may well keep off those sins which end in eternal suffering, as Holy Church teaches, and reasonably expect to avoid venial sin by our own effort. And if by our blindness and wretchedness we should at any time fall, we at once get up again, at the sweet touch of grace, and deliberately amend our lives by the teaching of Holy Church and according to the grievousness of the sin. And then we go out to God in love, neither, on the one hand, so abject that we seem to despair, nor, on the other, so confident as though we thought it did not matter. But we frankly admit our frailty for we realize that we could not stand for a moment apart from the keeping grace of God. And so we reverently cling to him, and trust him, and him alone. For God looks at things in one way, and man looks at them in another. It is natural for man humbly to accuse himself, and it is natural for the proper goodness of God graciously to excuse man. These are the two parts of the twofold sense in which the master regarded the fall of his beloved servant. The primary sense was the outward expression which was humble and gentle, compassionate and pitying, springing from endless love. Quite rightly does our Lord will that we should accuse ourselves, and recognize, deliberately and honestly, our fall and the harm that follows. And since we know that we can never make it good, we equally deliberately and honestly recognize his eternal love for us, and his abundant mercy. To have the grace to hold these both together is the humble self-accusation that our Lord asks of us; he himself works to that end in the lower part of our nature. It is shown in the expression on his face, which wears two aspects: one of sadness for man's fall, and the other of pleasure over the wonderful satisfaction he has made for men.

The second way in which the master looked was shown inwardly: it was more far reaching, and all of a piece. Such life and vigour as we have in the lower part of our nature spring from the higher part, coming down from our natural self-love through the grace of God. Between the two ways of the Master's looking there is no difference. The same single love pervades all. This blessed love works in us in two ways. In our lower part there are pains and passions, sympathy, pity, mercy and forgiveness, and so on – all most profitable; in the higher part are none of these, but altogether the most tremendous love and marvellous joy. And in this joy all our sufferings are put right. Here our Lord showed not only that we are excused from blame (this was when he regarded the higher part of our nature), but he also showed the honour and nobility to which he will bring us through the work of grace in the lower part of our nature, transforming our blameworthiness into eternal worthiness.

God in his kindness does not blame his elect, whose godly will never consented to sin; the mercy of God is necessarily joined to such, to maintain an element that can never be separated from him

53 THUS I saw that God's will is that we should realize how he does not regard the fall of a single one of his creatures to be saved more seriously than he regarded the fall of Adam. For Adam, as we know, was loved from eternity, and, securely kept in his time of need, is now happily restored to great and superlative joy. For our Lord is so good, so gentle, so considerate, that he never faults those who are going to bless and praise him for ever.

In all this that I have related, my desire was at least partly answered and my puzzlement somewhat eased by this loving, gracious revelation of the good Lord. Because of it I understood with absolute certainty that there is in every soul to be saved a godly will that never has assented to sin, and that never will. This will is so good that it never wills evil, but always wills good, and, in the sight of God, does good. Our Lord's will therefore is that we should know this by the Faith and our own belief, and in particular and in truth know that we have this blessed will safe and sound in our Lord Jesus Christ. For God is righteous, and it is therefore necessary that human nature – which is going to fill heaven – should be so joined and united to him, that it must have some substance that has never been and never can be separated from him. This has been achieved through his own good will and eternal and foreseeing purpose. Yet with all this joining and union, the redemption and repurchase of mankind is both necessary and urgent, and for the same reasons and purpose that Holy Church teaches us in our Faith.

I saw that God never *began* to love mankind: for just as mankind is going to enjoy unending bliss and thereby delight

God with regard to his handiwork, so, in the providence and intention of God, has mankind been known and loved from everlasting. For with the eternal consent and approval of the whole Trinity, the Second Person willed to become the foundation and the head of this lovely human nature. From him we come, with him we are included, to him we go, in him we shall find all heaven and lasting joy – all by the foreseeing purpose of the whole Trinity from before time. For before he made us he loved us, and when we were made we loved him. And this is a love made by the essential goodness of the Holy Spirit; a love that is mighty through the might of the Father, and wise through the wisdom of the Son. So man's soul is made by God, and in the same instant joined to God. I understand man's soul to be made. I mean, it is made, but made of nothing created. It is like this: when God was going to make man's body he took the dust of the earth – a matter which is a compound and collection of all sorts of material things – and with it he made man's body. But when he would make man's soul he took nothing: he just made it. Thus is created nature rightly united with its Maker who is essential nature and uncreated; in other words, God. From which it follows that there can be nothing at all between God and man's soul.

In this unending love man's soul is kept whole, as all these revelations are intended to show. In this unending love we too are led and kept by God, never to be lost. His will is that we should know that our soul is alive, and that through his goodness and grace this life will continue in heaven for ever, loving him, thanking him, praising him. And what we are going to be for ever, as such we have been treasured and hidden by God, known and loved from before time. Therefore he wants us to realize that the noblest thing he has ever made is mankind, and its complete expression and perfect example is the blessed soul of Christ. Moreover he would have us understand that his precious human soul was inseparably united to him when his humanity was made, and the union is so skilful and strong that this human soul is united to God, and thereby made holy for ever. More, he wills us to know that all souls to be saved in heaven for ever are joined and united in this union, and made holy in this holiness.

We are to rejoice that God and the soul mutually indwell each other; there is nothing between God and our soul: it is, so to speak, all God; through the work of the Holy Spirit, faith is the foundation of all the soul's virtues

54 AND because of his great and everlasting love for mankind, God makes no distinction in the love he has for the blessed soul of Christ and that which he has for the lowliest soul to be saved. It is easy enough to believe and trust that the blessed soul of Christ is pre-eminent in the glorious Godhead, and indeed, if I understand our Lord aright, where his blessed soul is there too, in substance, are all the souls which will be saved by him.

How greatly should we rejoice that God indwells our soul! Even more that our soul dwells in God! Our created soul is to be God's dwelling place: and the soul's dwelling place is to be God, who is uncreated. It is a great thing to know in our heart that God, our Maker, indwells our soul. Even greater is it to know that our soul, our created soul, dwells in the substance of God. Of that substance, God, are we what we are!

I could see no difference between God and our substance: it was all God, so to speak. Yet my mind understood that our substance was in God. In other words, God is God, and our substance his creation. For the almighty truth of the Trinity is our Father: he makes us and preserves us in himself; the deep wisdom of the Trinity is our Mother, in whom we are enfolded; the great goodness of the Trinity is our Lord, and we are enfolded by him too, and he by us. We are enfolded alike in the Father, in the Son, and in the Holy Spirit. And the Father is enfolded in us, the Son too, and the Holy Spirit as well: all mightiness, all wisdom, all goodness – one God, one Lord.

The virtue that is our faith springs from our basic nature and comes into our soul through the Holy Spirit. Through this virtue all virtues come to us, and without it no one can be virtuous. Our faith is nothing else but a right understanding, and true belief, and sure trust, that with regard to our essential being we are in God, and God in us, though we do not see him. This virtue, and all the others which spring from it, through the ordering of God, works great things in us. For Christ in his mercy works within us, and we graciously co-operate with him through the gift and power of the Holy Spirit. This makes us Christ's children, and Christian in our living.

Christ is our way, and leads and presents us to the Father; grace and mercy begin to work as soon as the soul is infused into the body; the Second Person took our sensuality into himself to save us from a twofold death

55 So Christ is our way, leading us surely in his laws. In his body he bears us up to heaven. I saw that Christ (who has within himself all who are to be saved) presents us in worship to his heavenly Father. And his Father most gratefully receives us, his present, and in his courtesy gives us back to his Son, Jesus Christ. Such an action and gift brings joy to the Father, and happiness to the Son, and delight to the Holy Spirit. And of all the things we do, that which delights our

Lord most is to see us rejoicing in the Holy Trinity's joy over our salvation. This is seen in the ninth revelation which deals more fully with the matter. Despite any feelings we may have of grief or pleasure, God wants us to realize by faith that we are in fact more in heaven than on earth. Our faith comes from the natural love of our soul, and the clear light of our reason, and the stability of our mind, given by God when he first made us. And when our soul was breathed into our body, and our senses began to work, at once mercy and grace began to work too, in pity and love caring for us and preserving us. In this work the Holy Spirit forms in our faith the hope that we shall come again to our substance who is above, to the virtue of Christ, developed and perfected through the Holy Spirit. In this way I understood that sensuality is founded in nature and mercy and grace. And such a foundation enables us to accept gifts that lead on to eternal life.

I saw with absolute certainty that our substance is in God, and, moreover, that he is in our sensuality too. The moment our soul was made sensual, at that moment was it destined from all eternity to be the City of God. And he shall come to that city, and never quit it. God never leaves the soul in which he dwells. This can be seen in what the sixteenth revelation says, 'the place that Jesus occupies in our soul he will never leave'. The gifts that God makes to his creatures he has given to his Son Jesus on our behalf. And he who indwells us retains these gifts until we are full grown in body and soul alike, each contributing its due share until by natural process we are spiritually mature. Then the natural foundation, with mercy's cooperation, will be inbreathed by the grace of the Holy Spirit with gifts that lead to eternal life.

Thus was my understanding led on by God to realize and to know that our own soul is a trinity – only created – like the blessed uncreated Trinity, and has been known and loved from before time, and, as I have already said, at its creation united to its Creator. This was a most satisfying and wonderful thing to behold, at once peaceful and reassuring, certain and delightful. Because of the wonderful union between soul and body wrought by God, it was necessary that man should be rescued from a twofold death. And this rescue could not be effected until the Second Person of the Trinity had taken into himself the lower part of human nature. The higher part was united at the earlier creation. Both were in Christ, higher and lower alike, and he is but one soul: the higher was united with God, peaceful, joyful, and blessed; the lower, sensuality, suffered for our salvation. These two parts were shown in the eighth revelation when my whole being was absorbed by the recollection and experience of Christ's passion and death. Even then there was a hint and inner awareness of the higher part, though at that time when it was shown I was unable to look up to heaven despite the proffered help. And that was because of the deep insight I was experiencing of the inner life, that life of high substance, that precious soul of Christ which is ever rejoicing in God.

It is easier to know God than the soul, for God is nearer; if we would know the soul we must seek God; his will is that we want to know about nature, mercy, and grace

56 So it came about that I was able to see with absolute certainty that it was easier for us to get to know God than to know our own soul. For our soul is so deeply set in God, and so greatly valued, that we cannot come to know it until we first know God, its Creator, to whom it is joined. All the same I saw that, for our own perfection, we must have a desire to know our soul with wisdom and accuracy. This will teach us to look for it where in fact it is: in God. And so by the gracious guidance of the Holy Spirit we come to know them both together.

Whether our urge is to know God or to know our own soul matters little: both are good and true.

God is nearer to us than our own soul, for he is the ground in which it stands, and he is the means by which substance and sensuality are so held together that they can never separate. Our soul reposes in God its true rest, and stands in God, its true strength, and is fundamentally rooted in God, its eternal love. So if we want to come to know our soul, and enjoy its fellowship as it were, it is necessary to seek it in our Lord God in whom it is enclosed. More of what I saw and understood of this enclosing I shall be speaking of when I come to the sixteenth revelation.

Our substance and our sensuality together are rightly named our soul, because they are united by God. That wonderful city, the seat of our Lord Jesus, is our sensuality in which he is enclosed, just as the substance of our nature is enclosed in him as with his blessed soul he sits at rest in the Godhead.

I saw quite clearly that with our longing should go penitence, until such time as we are led so deeply into God that we do in very truth know our own soul. It is our Lord himself who leads us into these lofty deeps with the self-same love that created us, and redeemed us through the mercy and grace of his blessed passion. All the same, we can never attain to the full knowledge of God until we have first known our own soul thoroughly. Until our soul reaches its full development we can never be completely holy; in other words, not until our sensuality has been raised to the level of our substance through the virtue of Christ's passion and enriched by all the trials laid upon us by our Lord in his mercy and grace.

I had, in part, received a touch of God – and it was fundamentally natural. For the foundation of our reason is in God, who is the substance of everything natural. Out of this essential nature spring mercy and grace spreading over us and bringing about all those things which make our happiness complete.

These are the foundation for our development and perfection. We have our life and our being in nature: we develop and reach fulfilment in mercy and grace. Goodness is one, but it has three qualities; and whenever one of them functions in our affairs all of them are called into action. God's purpose is that we should understand this and should have a fervent desire to get to know them more and more until we are made perfect. To know them thoroughly and to see them clearly – what else is this but the everlasting joy and blessedness awaiting us in heaven? God wills it to begin here, by coming to know his love. By reason alone we cannot advance, but only if there is in addition insight and love; nor are we going to be saved because God is the foundation of our nature, but only if, from the same source, we receive his mercy and grace. From the cooperation of these three (nature, mercy, grace) we obtain all our goodness. And first of all is natural good. When God created us he gave us much good, and then he gave a greater good still, which could only be received in our spirit. It was his foreseeing and purposeful wisdom that willed this twofold nature of ours.

In essence we are complete; we fail in our sensual nature; God heals it through his mercy and grace; the higher part of our nature is joined to God at our creation; Jesus our God is united to the lower part of our nature through his incarnation; virtues arise from faith; Mary is our Mother

57 WITH regard to our essential being, God made us so noble and rich that we always work in his will and for his honour. (I say 'we', but, of course, I am thinking of 'man-who-is-to-be-saved'.) I saw, indeed, that it is we whom he loved, and who always do what he approves, without limit. We are able to do this through our soul's share of the

wealth and great nobility given it when it was made one with our body. It is in this union that we have our sensuality.

As far as our essential nature goes we are complete. It is in the realm of our sensuality that we fail. This failing God will make good through the operation of mercy and grace which flows richly into us out of his own fundamental goodness. It is this goodness of his which makes mercy and grace work in us, and *our* natural goodness – given by God – enables us to accept it.

I saw that in God our nature is complete. There are different expressions of it, of which he is the source, all created to do his will. Their own nature preserves them, while mercy and grace restore and perfect them. None of these shall perish, for the higher part of our nature was united to God at our creation, and God united himself to our nature in its lower part when he became incarnate. In Christ therefore both parts are made one. For Christ means the Holy Trinity in whom our higher part is rooted and grounded; and he, the Second Person thereof, has taken our lower part, which had already been prepared for him. I saw clearly that all the works of God, past or future, were fully foreseen and known by him from before time was. For love he made mankind, and out of the same love he willed to become man.

The next 'good' that we receive is our faith, from which all our blessings stem. It springs from the wealth that our essential nature contributes to our sensitive soul, and it is planted in us, and we in it, through God's essential goodness working by mercy and grace. And so come all those other good things by which we are guided and saved.

For instance, the commandments of God are one of these 'goods'. We ought to understand these in two ways: there are his orders, which we must love and keep; and there are also his prohibitions: we ought to know them so that we hate and refuse them. These two ways include all we do.

Or there are the seven sacraments, each following the other in God-appointed order. Or virtue of any sort. The very virtues which rise through the goodness of God out of our essential nature, are given by the Holy Spirit, working in mercy, restoring through grace. These virtues and gifts are our treasure in Jesus Christ. For when God united himself to our humanity in the Virgin's womb he took also our sensual soul. When he took it – having included us all in himself – he united it to our essential nature. In this uniting he was perfect man, for Christ who unites with himself every one who is to be saved is perfect man. So our Lady is *our* Mother too and, in Christ, we are incorporated in her, and born of her. She who is the Mother of our Saviour is Mother of all who are to be saved in our Saviour. Indeed, our Saviour himself is our Mother for we are for ever being born of him, and shall never be delivered!

All this was made abundantly and beautifully clear. It is referred to in the first revelation where it is said, 'We are all enfolded in him and he in us.' And the inclusion is mentioned in the sixteenth revelation where he is spoken of as 'seated in our soul'. It is his pleasure and bliss to reign in our intelligence and to sit at ease in our soul, dwelling there eternally, working us all into himself. In this task he wants us to help him, giving him our whole attention, learning his lessons, keeping his laws, wanting all that he does to be achieved, and really trusting him. I saw indeed that our essential being is in God!

God is never displeased with the wife he has chosen; three attributes
of the Trinity: fatherhood, motherhood, and lordship; our
essence is in each Person, but our sensual nature in Christ alone

58 GOD the blessed Trinity is everlasting Being. Just as he is eternal, without beginning, so has his purpose been eternal, namely to make mankind. This fine nature was

prepared in the first instance for his own Son, the Second Person. And when he so willed, with the concurrence of each Person of the Trinity, he made all of us at one and the same time. When he made us he joined and united us to himself. By such union we are kept as pure and noble as when we were first made. It is because of this most precious union that we can love our Maker, please him and praise him, thank him and rejoice in him for ever. And this is the plan continually at work in every soul to be saved – the divine will that I have already mentioned. So when he made us God almighty was our kindly Father, and God all-wise our kindly Mother, and the Holy Spirit their love and goodness; all one God, one Lord. In this uniting together he is our real, true husband, and we his loved wife and sweetheart. He is never displeased with his wife! 'I love you and you love me,' he says, 'and our love will never be broken.'

I saw the blessed Trinity working. I saw that there were these three attributes: fatherhood, motherhood, and lordship – all in one God. In the almighty Father we have been sustained and blessed with regard to our created natural being from before all time. By the skill and wisdom of the Second Person we are sustained, restored, and saved with regard to our sensual nature, for he is our Mother, Brother, and Saviour. In our good Lord the Holy Spirit we have, after our life and hardship is over, that reward and rest which surpasses for ever any and everything we can possibly desire – such is his abounding grace and magnificent courtesy.

Our life too is threefold. In the first stage we have our being, in the second our growth, and in the third our perfection. The first is nature, the second mercy, and the third grace. For the first I realized that the great power of the Trinity is our Father, the deep wisdom our Mother, and the great love our Lord. All this we have by nature and in our created and essential being. Moreover I saw that the Second Person who is our

Mother with regard to our essential nature, that same dear Person has become our Mother in the matter of our sensual nature. We are God's creation twice: essential being and sensual nature. Our being is that higher part which we have in our Father, God almighty, and the Second Person of the Trinity is Mother of this basic nature, providing the substance in which we are rooted and grounded. But he is our Mother also in mercy, since he has taken our sensual nature upon himself. Thus 'our Mother' describes the different ways in which he works, ways which are separate to us, but held together in him. In our Mother, Christ, we grow and develop; in his mercy he reforms and restores us; through his passion, death, and resurrection he has united us to our being. So does our Mother work in mercy for all his children who respond to him and obey him.

Grace works with mercy too, and especially in two ways. The work is that of the Third Person, the Holy Spirit, who works by *rewarding* and *giving*. Rewarding is the generous gift of truth that the Lord makes to him who has suffered. Giving is a magnanimous gesture which he makes freely by his grace: perfect, and far beyond the deserts of any of his creatures.

Thus in our Father, God almighty, we have our being. In our merciful Mother we have reformation and renewal, and our separate parts are integrated into perfect man. In yielding to the gracious impulse of the Holy Spirit we are made perfect. Our essence is in our Father, God almighty, and in our Mother, God all-wise, and in our Lord the Holy Spirit, God all-good. Our essential nature is entire in each Person of the Trinity, who is one God. Our sensual nature is in the Second Person alone, Jesus Christ. In him is the Father too, and the Holy Spirit. In and by him have we been taken out of hell with a strong arm; and out of earth's wretchedness have been wonderfully raised to heaven, and united, most blessedly, to him who is our true being. And we have developed in spiritual wealth and character through all Christ's virtues, and by the gracious work of the Holy Spirit.

In the elect, wickedness is transformed into blessedness by the work of mercy and grace; God's way is to set good against evil by Jesus, our Mother in grace; the most virtuous soul is the most humble; all virtues are grounded in God

59 ALL this blessedness is ours through mercy and grace. We would never have had it or known it if goodness (that is, God) had not been opposed. It is because of this that we enjoy this bliss. Wickedness was allowed to rise up against goodness, and the goodness of mercy and grace rose up against wickedness and then turned it all into goodness and honour, at least as far as those who are to be saved are concerned. For it is the way of God to set good against evil. So Jesus Christ who sets good against evil is our real Mother. We owe our being to him – and this is the essence of motherhood! – and all the delightful, loving protection which ever follows. God is as really our Mother as he is our Father. He showed this throughout, and particularly when he said that sweet word, 'It is I.' In other words, 'It is I who am the strength and goodness of Fatherhood; I who am the wisdom of Motherhood; I who am light and grace and blessed love; I who am Trinity; I who am Unity; I who am the sovereign goodness of every single thing; I who enable you to love; I who enable you to long. It is I, the eternal satisfaction of every genuine desire.'

For the soul is at its best, its most noble and honourable, when it is most lowly, and humble, and gentle. Springing from this fundamental source and as part of our natural endowment, are all the virtues of our sensual nature, aided and abetted as they are by mercy and grace. Without such assistance we should be in a poor way!

Our great Father, God almighty, who is Being, knew and loved us from eternity. Through his knowledge, and in the marvellous depths of his charity, together with the foresight and wisdom of the whole blessed Trinity, he willed that the Second Person should become our Mother, Brother, and Saviour. Hence it follows that God is as truly our Mother as he is our Father. Our Father decides, our Mother works, our good Lord, the Holy Spirit, strengthens. So we ought to love our God in whom we have our own being, reverently thanking him, and praising him for creating us, earnestly beseeching our Mother for mercy and pity, and our Lord, the Spirit, for help and grace. For in these three is contained our life: nature, mercy, grace. From these we get our humility, gentleness, patience and pity. From them too we get our hatred of sin and wickedness – it is the function of virtue to hate these.

So we see that Jesus is the true Mother of our nature, for he made us. He is our Mother, too, by grace, because he took our created nature upon himself. All the lovely deeds and tender services that beloved motherhood implies are appropriate to the Second Person. In him the godly will is always safe and sound, both in nature and grace, because of his own fundamental goodness. I came to realize that there were three ways of looking at God's motherhood: the first is based on the fact that our nature is *made*; the second is found in the assumption of that nature – there begins the motherhood of grace; the third is the motherhood of work which flows out over all by that same grace – the length and breadth and height and depth of it is everlasting. And so is his love.

We are brought back and fulfilled by the mercy and grace of our
sweet, kind, and ever-loving Mother Jesus; the attributes of
motherhood; Jesus, our true Mother, feeds us not with milk but
with himself, opening his side to us, and calling out all our love

60 BUT now I must say a little more about this 'over-flowing' as I understand its meaning: how we have been brought back again by the motherhood of mercy and grace to that natural condition which was ours originally when we were made through the motherhood of natural love – which love, indeed, has never left us.

Our Mother by nature and grace – for he would become our Mother in everything – laid the foundation of his work in the Virgin's womb with great and gentle condescension. (This was shown in the first revelation when I received a mental picture of the Virgin's genuine simplicity at the time she conceived.) In other words, it was in this lowly place that God most high, the supreme wisdom of all, adorned and arrayed himself with our poor flesh, ready to function and serve as Mother in all things.

A mother's is the most intimate, willing, and dependable of all services, because it is the truest of all. None has been able to fulfil it properly but Christ, and he alone can. We know that our own mother's bearing of us was a bearing to pain and death, but what does Jesus, our true Mother, do? Why, he, All-love, bears us to joy and eternal life! Blessings on him! Thus he carries us within himself in love. And he is in labour until the time has fully come for him to suffer the sharpest pangs and most appalling pain possible – and in the end he dies. And not even when this is over, and we ourselves have been born to eternal bliss, is his marvellous love completely satisfied. This he shows in that overwhelming word of love,

'If I could possibly have suffered more, indeed I would have done so.'

He might die no more, but that does not stop him working, for he needs to feed us ... it is an obligation of his dear, motherly, love. The human mother will suckle her child with her own milk, but our beloved Mother, Jesus, feeds us with himself, and, with the most tender courtesy, does it by means of the Blessed Sacrament, the precious food of all true life. And he keeps us going through his mercy and grace by all the sacraments. This is what he meant when he said, 'It is I whom Holy Church preaches and teaches.' In other words, 'All the health and life of sacraments, all the virtue and grace of my word, all the goodness laid up for you in Holy Church – it is I.' The human mother may put her child tenderly to her breast, but our tender Mother Jesus simply leads us into his blessed breast through his open side, and there gives us a glimpse of the Godhead and heavenly joy – the inner certainty of eternal bliss. The tenth ★ revelation showed this, and said as much with that word, 'See how I love you', as looking into his side he rejoiced.

This fine and lovely word *Mother* is so sweet and so much its own that it cannot properly be used of any but him, and of her who is his own true Mother – and ours. In essence *motherhood* means love and kindness, wisdom, knowledge, goodness. Though in comparison with our spiritual birth our physical birth is a small, unimportant, straightforward sort of thing, it still remains that it is only through his working that it can be done at all by his creatures. A kind, loving mother who understands and knows the needs of her child will look after it tenderly just because it is the nature of a mother to do so. As the child grows older she changes her methods – but not her love. Older still, she allows the child to be punished so that

★ Sloane 2499 has 'IX', which is obviously an uncorrected slip of the pen.

its faults are corrected and its virtues and graces developed. This way of doing things, with much else that is right and good, is our Lord at work in those who are doing them. Thus he is our Mother in nature, working by his grace in our lower part, for the sake of the higher. It is his will that we should know this, for he wants all our love to be fastened on himself. Like this I could see that our indebtedness, under God, to fatherhood and motherhood – whether it be human or divine – is fully met in truly loving God. And this blessed love Christ himself produces in us. This was shown in all the revelations, and especially in those splendid words that he uttered, 'It is I whom you love.'

The tenderness of Jesus at our spiritual birth; though he allows us to fall in order to know our wretchedness, he swiftly lifts us up; he does not cease loving us for all our sin; he will not allow his child to perish; he wants us to be childlike, and fly to him in our need

61 IN the matter of our spiritual birth he preserves us with infinitely greater tenderness, since our soul is so much more valuable in his sight. He kindles our understanding, he directs our paths, he eases our consciences, he comforts our soul, he lightens our heart. He gives us – partially at least – knowledge and trust in his blessed Godhead, while at the same time we remember his manhood and passion, and have a proper wonder at his superlative goodness. He makes us love whatever he loves for love of him, and to find in himself and his works our ample reward. If we fall he catches us lovingly in his gracious embrace and swiftly raises us. Strengthened in this fashion by his working in us we freely choose to serve him and to love him, by his grace, world without end.

And then he allows some of us to fall more severely and painfully than ever before – or so it seems to us. And then we (not all of whom are wise), think it was a waste of time to have started at all. It is not so, of course. We need to fall, and we need to realize this. If we never fell we should never know how weak and wretched we are in ourselves; nor should we fully appreciate the astonishing love of our Maker. In heaven we shall really and eternally see that we sinned grievously in this life: yet despite all this, we shall also see that it made no difference at all to his love, and we were no less precious in his sight. By the simple fact that we fell we shall gain a deep and wonderful knowledge of what God's love means. Love that cannot, will not, be broken by sin, is rock-like, and quite astonishing. It is a good thing to know this. Another benefit is the sense of insignificance and humbling that we get by see-ing ourselves fall. Through it, as we know, we shall be raised up to heaven: but such exaltation might never have been ours without the prior humbling. We have *got* to see this. If we do not, no fall would do us any good. Normally we fall first, and see afterwards – and both through God's mercy.

A mother may allow her child sometimes to fall, and to learn the hard way, for its own good. But because she loves the child she will never allow the situation to become dangerous. Admittedly earthly mothers have been known to let their children die, but our heavenly Mother, Jesus, will never let us, his children, die. He and none but he is almighty, all wisdom, all love. Blessings on him! But often when we are shown the extent of our fall and wretchedness we are so scared and dread-fully ashamed that we scarcely know where to look. But our patient Mother does not want us to run away: nothing would be more displeasing to him. His desire is that we should do what a child does: for when a child is in trouble or is scared it runs to mother for help as fast as it can. Which is what he wants us to do, saying with the humility of a child, 'Kind, thoughtful, dearest Mother, do be sorry for me. I have got myself into a filthy mess, and am not a bit like you. I cannot begin to put it right without your special and willing help.' Even if we do not feel immediate relief we can still be sure that he behaves like a wise mother. If he sees it is better for us to mourn and weep he lets us do so – with pity and sympathy, of course, and for the right length of time – because he loves us. And he wants us to copy the child who always and naturally trusts mother's love through thick and thin.

Moreover he wills that we should hold tight to the Faith of Holy Church, and find there in that Communion of Saints our dearest Mother, who comforts us because she really understands. Individuals may often break down – or so it seems to them – but the whole body of Holy Church is unbreakable, whether in the past, present, or future. So it is a good, sound, grace-bringing thing to resolve, humbly but firmly, to be fastened and united to Holy Church our Mother, – in other words, to Jesus Christ. For the merciful ample flood of his precious blood and water suffices to make us sweet and clean; the Saviour's blessed wounds are open, and rejoice to heal us; the dear, gracious hands of our Mother are ever about us, and eager to help.

In all this work he functions as a kindly nurse who has no other business than to care for the well-being of her charge. It is his business to save us; it is his glory to do this for us; and it is his will that we should know it. For it is also his will that we should love him dearly, and trust him humbly and wholeheartedly. All this he showed in those gracious words, 'I will keep you safe and sound.'

God's love never lets his chosen lag behind; all their trouble is transformed into everlasting joy; we are dependent on God both for nature and grace; every variety of nature is in man; we need not seek the different varieties: we must seek Holy Church

62 AT that time I was shown our frailty and our falls, our breakdowns and our ineffectiveness, our hurt pride and our rejection, and all the woes that I thought could possibly happen to us in this life. At the same time he showed his blessed power, wisdom, and love. By these he keeps us just as tenderly, gently, and surely when the going is hard, as he does when we are experiencing comfort and consolation. He does it for his own glory's sake, and for our salvation. So he exalts us spiritually to heaven, and turns all to his glory and to our eternal joy. His love never lets us lag behind.

All this is due to God's innate goodness, and comes to us by the operation of his grace. God is kind because it is his nature. Goodness-by-nature implies God. He is the foundation, the substance, the thing itself, what it is by nature. He is the true Father and Mother of what things are by nature. Every kind of 'nature' that he has caused to flow out of himself to fulfil his purpose will be brought back and restored to him when man is saved by the work of grace. For all the varied natures he has implanted in different creatures are only partly complete. In man alone is the whole, full and powerful, beautiful and good, regal and noble, grave, precious, and glorious. Here we can see that we depend upon God for our nature, just as we do for grace. Here too we can see that we have no great need to go out in search of the different varieties. No further than Holy Church, in fact, our Mother's breast. Or, in other words, our own soul, the home of our Lord. There we shall find all. We find it now through faith and reason: we shall find it hereafter in our Lord himself, in truth, without doubt, and in heaven. But no man or woman should take this to refer to himself in particular. That would be a mistake. The general reference is to our precious Christ. For him was this fair nature prepared; for the glory and splendour of man's creation; for the joy and blessedness of man's salvation . . . all just as he saw, understood, and knew from the first.

Sin is more vile and painful than hell; it hurts nature but grace rescues it and destroys sin; not all the children of Jesus are born yet; on earth we are still weak children, but in heaven there are joys ever new, and never ending

63 HERE, too, we can see that we can really hate sin by nature, and really hate sin by grace. In itself nature is good and fair, and to save it, and to destroy sin, grace was sent: to bring fair nature back to the blessedness from which it began, to God; only now with the added dignity and worth that came from the powerful operation of grace. For in the presence of God and all his holy ones it will be seen as a matter of eternal joy that nature has been tried in the fires of affliction, and that no fault or imperfection has been found in it. Nature and grace are agreed, for both are of God. He works in these two ways, and loves in one. Neither grace nor nature work independently of each other, nor can they ever be separated.

When we by God's mercy and help agree with nature and grace we shall see in very truth that sin is more vile and painful than hell itself. Indeed there is no comparison: sin contradicts our nature. For just as sin is really unclean, so is it really unnatural, and therefore is a horrible thing for the beloved soul to see when, taught by nature and grace, it would be beautiful and shining in the sight of God.

We need have no fear of this, unless it is the kind of fear that urges us on. But we make our humble complaint to our beloved Mother, and he sprinkles us with his precious blood, and makes our soul pliable and tender, and restores us to our full beauty in course of time. This is his glory and our eternal joy. And this sweet and lovely work he will never cease from doing until all his beloved children are born and delivered. This was showed in the explanation of his spiritual thirst, that longing that loves and lasts until the Day of Judgement.

Thus in Jesus, our true Mother, has our life been grounded, through his own uncreated foresight, and the Father's almighty power, and the exalted and sovereign goodness of the Holy Spirit. In taking our nature he restored us to life; in his blessed death upon the cross he bore us to eternal life; and now, since then, and until the Day of Judgement, he feeds and helps us on – just as one would expect the supreme and royal nature of motherhood to act, and the natural needs of childhood to require.

Beautiful and sweet is our heavenly Mother in the sight of our souls; and, in the sight of our heavenly Mother, dear and lovely are the gracious children; gentle and humble, with all the lovely natural qualities of children. The natural child does not despair of mother's love; the natural child does not give itself airs; the natural child loves mother, and the other children. These are beautiful qualities, and there are many others as well, and with them all our heavenly Mother is served and pleased. And I understood that there is no higher state in this life than that of childhood, because of our inadequate and feeble capacity and intellect, until such time as our gracious Mother shall bring us up to our Father's bliss. And then the true meaning of those lovely words will be made known to us, 'It is all going to be all right. You will see for yourself that everything is going to be all right.' And then shall the blessedness of our motherhood in Christ begin anew in the joys of our God: a new beginning and an eternal one. To this new beginning all his blessed children born to him by nature shall be brought to him again by grace.

The fifteenth revelation: the absence of God in this life gives us very great pain and trouble; we shall suddenly be taken from all our pain; Jesus is our Mother; God is very pleased with our patient waiting; his will is that we bear our discomfort lightly for love of him, mindful of the day of deliverance

64 BEFORE this I had had a great and longing desire that God should give me deliverance from this life. I had often considered the woes of this present world, and the joys and blessedness of the future. Even if there had been no suffering in this life, but no Lord either, I sometimes thought it would have been more than I could have borne. This grieved me, and made me long all the more eagerly. Besides, because of my own wretchedness, slothfulness, and incapacity, I did not want to live and toil as it fell to me to do.

To all this our Lord in his courtesy gave an answer that brought comfort and patience. He said, 'Suddenly you will be taken from all your pain, all your sickness, all your discomfort, and all your woe. You will come up above, with me as your reward, and you will be filled to the full with love and blessedness. Never again will there be any sort of suffering, or unhappiness, or failure of will. It will be all joy and bliss eternally. Why should it grieve you to suffer a while, seeing that this is my will and my glory?'

In this word, 'Suddenly you will be taken', I saw that God rewards man for his patience in waiting on God's will and God's time, and for extending that patience over the whole span of life. Not to know the time of one's passing is a very good thing: if a man knew it, he would not wait patiently for it. It is the will of God that while the soul is in the body it should always seem to itself to be at the point of being taken. All this living and waiting here is but a moment: when we are taken suddenly out of suffering into bliss, the suffering will be nothing.

At this time I saw a body lying on the earth, heavy and ugly, without shape or form, a swollen mass of stinking filth. And suddenly out of this body sprang a most beautiful creature, a little child, perfectly shaped and formed, active and lively, whiter than a lily: and he quickly glided up to heaven. The swollen body stood for the great misery of our mortal flesh, and the little child for the clean and pure soul. I thought, 'With this body this child's beauty cannot live, and on this child no physical filth can stay.'

It is more blessed for man to be taken from suffering than for suffering to be taken from man, for if suffering be taken from us it may come back. It is therefore a very great consolation for a loving soul to consider that we shall be taken away from suffering. I saw in this promise our Lord's marvellous compassion for us in our woe, and his kind pledge of complete deliverance. He wills us to be comforted with such superabundance, as he showed in his words, 'You will come up above, with me as your reward, and you will be filled to the full with love and blessedness.'

God's will is that we should concentrate on this blessed consideration as often as possible – and by his grace stay with it as long as we can. This is a blessed thing for the soul that is led of God to contemplate, and greatly honouring to him all the time it lasts. If, because of our weakness, we fall back again into our old inertia and spiritual blindness, and experience suffering both spiritual and physical, God's will is for us to know that he has not forgotten us. This is what he means in those words said to comfort us, 'Never again will there be any sort of suffering, or sickness, or unhappiness, or failure of will. It will be all joy and bliss eternally. Why should it grieve you to suffer awhile, seeing that this is my will and my glory?'

It is God's will that we should take his promises and his consolations as generously and comprehensively as we can, and at the same time take the waiting and the discomfort as casually as possible, as mere nothings. The more casually we take them, and the less store we set by them for love of him, the less will be the pain we experience, and the greater our thanks and reward.

He who chooses God out of love and with reverent humility is sure to be saved; this reverent humility sees the Lord to be astonishingly great, and itself to be astonishingly small; God's will is that we fear nothing but himself; power over the enemy is held in our Friend's hand; therefore all that God does gives us great delight

65 So I came to understand that the man or woman who chooses God deliberately in this life out of love may be sure that he is loved for ever. And it is grace that produces that eternal love in him. For God wills that we should hold confidently on to this so that here below we may be as sure of our hope of heavenly bliss as we shall be absolutely certain of it when we are there above. The greater pleasure and joy we have in this confidence, with due humility and reverence, of course, the better he likes it, as it was showed. The *reverence* I am meaning is a holy, proper, fear of our Lord, coupled with humility. In other words that the creature sees the Lord to be astonishingly great, and itself to be astonishingly small.

These virtues are the eternal possession of the beloved of God. To some extent they may be seen and experienced even now when the gracious presence of the Lord is felt. His presence in all things is something most to be desired, for it produces a wonderful certainty when there is true faith, and gives a sure hope (because of his great charity) and an awe that is sweet and delightful. It is God's will that I see myself as much bound in loving gratitude to him as if all that he had ever done had been done for me alone. In his heart every one should think thus of his Lover. The charity of God makes such a unity within us that when it is seen for what it is in truth no one can separate himself from anyone else. So ought our soul to reckon that God has done for us alone all that he has ever done.

And he shows us this to make us love him, and to fear none but him. It is his will that we understand that all the power of our enemy is held in our Friend's hand. So the soul that is quite sure of this fears none but him whom it loves. Any other fear it ascribes to the emotions or physical sickness or to the imagination. Therefore, though we may be in such pain, trouble, and distress that it seems that we can think of nothing else but our own sorry plight, as soon as may be we should pass lightly over it, and regard it as a mere nothing. Why? Because God wills us to know that if we know him and love him and reverently fear him we shall have great peace and rest, and whatever he does will give us great pleasure. Which is what our Lord was showing when he said, 'Why should it grieve you to suffer awhile, seeing that this is my will and my glory?'

Now I have told you of fifteen revelations which God was kind enough to put into my mind, and which have been renewed by the subsequent enlightenment and touch of the same Spirit (I hope) that showed me them all. The first of the fifteen revelations began early in the morning, about four o'clock, and they went steadily on in regular and due order until it was past nine.

*The sixteenth revelation concludes and confirms the previous fifteen;
Julian's frailty and mourning; her flippant speech after all
Jesus' great comfort, when she said she had raved – seeing she
was so ill, I suppose it was only a venial sin; the Devil afterwards powerfully afflicts her, and nearly kills her*

66 THE following night our good Lord showed me the
sixteenth revelation as I shall be telling. And this sixteenth concluded and confirmed all the previous fifteen.

But first of all I must tell you about my weakness, wretchedness, and blindness. I said at the beginning, 'Suddenly all my
pain was taken from me', and in fact I had no pain to trouble
or distress me all the while the fifteen revelations lasted. But at
the end, everything closed up and I saw no more. At one
moment I was feeling that I was going to survive, and at the
next my sickness had returned, first in my head which
began to throb, and then suddenly my whole body felt as ill
as it had ever been. I was as stupid and bereft as if I had not
had a grain of comfort. Wretch that I was, I moaned and cried
as I became aware of my bodily pains and lack of comfort,
both spiritual and physical.

Then came a religious person to me and asked me how I
was doing. I said I had raved today. And he laughed loud and
heartily. And I said, 'The cross that stood before my face – I
thought it was bleeding freely.' At this the person I was
speaking to became quite serious, and surprised. And I felt
very ashamed and amazed at my thoughtlessness, and I
thought, 'The man takes my least word seriously', so I said
no more about it. When I saw how seriously he took it and
with what respect, I wept, feeling much ashamed. I should
have liked to receive absolution, but it was no time for talking
to a priest about it, for I thought to myself, 'Why should a
priest believe *me*? I am not believing our Lord God.' Yet I had

truly believed all the while I had seen him, and in intention I had meant to do so for ever, but fool that I was, I let it slip from my mind. What a wretch I am! A great sin it was and most unkind, that, because of the foolishness of a little pain, I should be so stupid as to lose temporarily all the comfort that this blessed revelation from God had brought. You can see what sort of person I am! But our Lord, ever courteous, did not leave me, and so I lay quietly till night time trusting in his mercy. Then I fell asleep.

And in my sleep, at the beginning, I thought the Fiend had me by the throat, putting his face very near mine. It was like a young man's face, and long and extraordinarily lean: I never saw the like. The colour was the red of a tilestone newly fired, and there were black spots like freckles, dirtier than the tilestone. His hair was rust red, clipped in front, with side-locks hanging over his cheeks. He grinned at me with sly grimace, thereby revealing white teeth, which made it, I thought, all the more horrible. There was no proper shape to his body or hands, but with his paws he held me by the throat and would have strangled me if he could.

This ugly revelation was made while I was asleep, unlike any of the others. But all the time I went on trusting I would be saved and kept by the mercy of God. And our Lord in his courtesy gave me the grace to wake up.

I was barely alive. The people around me saw, and started to bathe my temples, and my heart began to revive. And then a light smoke came through the door, with great heat and filthy smell. I said, 'Benedicite Domine! The whole place is on fire!' I thought it was a real fire that would burn us all to death. I asked those around me if they noticed the stench. 'No,' said they, 'they noticed nothing.' 'Blessed be God,' said I, for then I knew that it was the Fiend who had come to torment me. And at once I recalled what our Lord had showed me that very day, together with all the Faith of Holy Church – it was all one to my sight – and to that I fled for comfort. And then it all vanished, and I was left in a great peace and rest, sick no more in body, and fearful no longer in conscience.

The glorious city of the soul; made so nobly, it cannot be better made; the Trinity rejoices over it eternally; the soul finds rest in none but God, whose seat is in the soul, and who rules all things

67 THEN our Lord opened my spiritual eyes, and showed me the soul in the middle of my heart. The soul was as large as if it were an eternal world, and a blessed kingdom as well. Its condition showed it to be a most glorious city. In the midst of it sat our Lord Jesus, God and Man, beautiful in person, and great in stature, the greatest of bishops, most majestic of kings, and most worshipful Lord. And I saw him arrayed in solemn state. Most gloriously is he seated within the soul, in rightful peace and rest. His Godhead rules and upholds both heaven and earth, and all that is, and is supreme in might, wisdom, and goodness. Nor will he quit the place he holds in our soul for ever – as I see it. For in us is he completely at home, and has his eternal dwelling.

In this he showed the deep satisfaction that he has in making man's soul. The Father might well create, the Son could well create, the Holy Spirit would well create Man's soul. And so it was done. And so it is that the Blessed Trinity rejoices for ever in the making of man's soul. Before time was he saw what he would ever delight in. Everything he has made reveals his Lordship. Understanding of this was given by the illustration of the man who was permitted to see the great distinctions and kingdoms possessed by a prince. When he had seen all the lesser treasures he was, still marvelling, moved to seek higher for the prince's home itself, knowing, quite rightly, that that would be the most glorious place of all. And so I came to understand the truth that our soul can never find its rest in lesser things. When it is lifted above created things and turns to itself, it cannot keep on gazing at itself but all its gaze is set blessedly on God its Maker who dwells therein. For man's soul is God's true dwelling. The greatest light that shines most brightly in that city is, as I see it, the glorious love of our Lord. What more can make us rejoice in God than to see that he rejoices in us the highest of all his works? For I saw in the same revelation that if the blessed Trinity could have made man's soul better, fairer, nobler than he did, he would not have been, as he was, fully satisfied with the making of his soul. And he wills that our hearts be lifted high above earthly depths and empty sorrows and rejoice in him.

The certain confidence that it was Jesus who showed all these things, and that she did not rave; we must have some trust that in all our troubles we shall not be overcome

68 I FOUND the sight of this revelation both delightful and restful, as indeed it will be in eternity. That we should see this here and now is most pleasing to God, and very beneficial to ourselves. It makes the soul that sees this become like him whom it sees, and by his grace it quietly unites it to him in peace. The fact that I saw him *sitting* gave me particular happiness, for *sitting* means sure confidence and that in turn implies an eternal dwelling-place.

And he gave me to understand for certain that it was he who had showed me all I had seen previously. When I had given this my close attention our good Lord spoke quietly without voice or word of mouth – just as he had done before – and said so sweetly, 'You know well enough that it was no raving that you saw today. But take it: believe it: hold on to it:

comfort yourself with it and trust it. You will not be overcome.'

These last words were added to ensure that I believed it was our Lord Jesus who had showed me all this. Just as in his first word our Lord said, with his blessed passion in mind, 'In this way is the Devil overcome,' so now in this last word he says with complete assurance – and he means us all – 'You will not be overcome.' All this trusting in the real comfort is meant to be taken generally, for it applies to all my fellow Christians, as I have said before. It is God's will. This word, 'You will not be overcome' was said very distinctly and firmly to give us confidence and comfort for whatever troubles may come. He did not say, 'You will never have a rough passage, you will never be over-strained, you will never feel uncomfortable', but he *did* say, 'You will never be overcome.' God wants us to pay attention to these words, so as to trust him always with strong confidence, through thick and thin. For he loves us, and delights in us; so he wills that we should love and delight in him in return, and trust him with all our strength. So all will be well.

And then he vanished, and I saw no more.

The second long temptation of the Devil to despair; Julian firmly trusts in God, and in the Faith of Holy Church; she goes back to the passion of Christ, by which she has been delivered

69 AND again the Fiend came with heat and stench, and kept me fully occupied coping with him, so foul and nauseating was his stench, so frightful and unbearable. And I could hear a distinct chattering, as if two people were talking; it seemed to me that both were chattering away at once, discussing something with great earnestness. But they muttered so quietly that I could not understand what they were saying.

This was calculated to drive me to despair, or so I thought. They seemed to me to be like those who mock the telling of the beads * when they are said aloud with the mouth only, without the devotion, attention, and due care which we owe to God when we say our prayers.

And our Lord God gave me grace to trust him with all my strength, and to comfort my soul by speaking aloud – as I might have done to another person in similar straits. Yet I thought that this 'business' was unlike any other sort of business I knew.

I turned my eyes again to the same cross which had been my comfort previously; my tongue I occupied with talk of Christ's passion, with repeating the creed of Holy Church; and my heart I fixed on God with all my trust and strength. And I thought to myself, 'You have been much occupied keeping yourself in the Faith lest you should be caught by the enemy. If from now on you were to be equally occupied keeping yourself from sin, that would be a supremely good thing!' And I thought, 'If, in truth, I were safe from sin, I would be safe also from the fiends of hell and the enemies of my soul.'

Thus did the Fiend keep me busy all through the night until nine o'clock the following morning. And then all was over and gone. Nothing remained but the smell, which still lasted a while. And I despised him. So it was that I was delivered by virtue of Christ's passion, for 'in this way is the Fiend overcome', as our Lord Jesus Christ had said earlier.

* i.e. the recitation of the rosary, a method of praying which makes use of a string of beads.

In all our troubles we have to be steadfast in the truth, and firmly trust in God; if our faith is unopposed it deserves no reward; all these revelations agree with the Faith

70 IN this revelation our Lord made me realize that the sight of it would pass, but that its substance the faith would keep, and that through his own good will and grace. For he left me neither sign nor token whereby I might know its reality, but he did leave with me his own blessed word and understanding of its truth, and bade me emphatically to believe it. And so I do; blessed be God! I believe it was our Saviour who revealed it, and that it was the Faith that he revealed; and so I believe it, and rejoice. And I am bound to it, and to his interpretation of it, according to the words which follow, 'hold on to it: comfort yourself with it: and trust it.' I am bound therefore to keep believing in it.

Yet on the very day that it happened, when the vision had passed, I – wretch that I am! – denied it, and said quite openly that I had raved. But mercifully our Lord Jesus would not let it disappear, but showed it all over again within my soul in greater detail, lighting it up by his precious love. He said, with great emphasis, yet quietly, 'You know well enough that it was no raving that you saw today.' As if to say 'The fact that the vision passed from you meant that you had lost it, and could not hold on to it. But understand it now' – meaning, of course, 'now that you are seeing it'. This was intended not merely for that particular occasion but also as a basis for my faith, for he at once went on to say, 'take it: believe it: hold on to it: comfort yourself with it: and trust it. You will not be overcome.'

In the words that follow 'Take it', his intention is to fix it faithfully in our heart. For his will is that we should continue to believe it to the end of our life, and remain in the fullness of this joy thereafter. He wants us always to trust his blessed promise wholeheartedly, knowing, as we do, his goodness. For our faith is variously opposed by our own blindness and by our spiritual enemies, within and without. So our most dear Lover helps us by giving us spiritual insight and true doctrine; and he gives them in different ways, both externally and internally, in order that we may know him. Whatever his manner of teaching, his will is that we should be wise enough to perceive him, gentle enough to receive him, and faithful enough to keep ourselves in him. For there can be no goodness in this life above and apart from our Faith, and no spiritual help in anything less: so it seems to me. But *in* the Faith is where our Lord wills us to stay. It is by his work and goodness that we have to keep ourselves in it; and it is by his permission that we are tested therein by our spiritual foes, and are made strong. For if our faith met no opposition it would deserve no reward, if I understand our Lord's meaning aright.

Jesus' will is that our souls should look gladly at him, just as he looks at us cheerfully and lovingly; his countenance wears three expressions, that of his passion, that of his sympathy, and that of his blessedness

71 GLAD, merry, and sweet is the blessed and lovely face that our Lord shows to our soul. He is ever turned towards us who live in longing love. And he wants our soul to respond cheerfully to him, which is no less than he deserves. In this way I hope his grace will continue to bring our outward expression more and more into line with our inner looks: to unite us all with him and with one another in the true and lasting joy that is Jesus.

I understand the countenance of our Lord to have three

kinds of expression. The first is the look on his face at his passion, which was shown while he was still alive though dying. His looks then were mournful and sorrowful, yet at the same time they were glad and cheerful, for he is God. The second look is one of tender pity and compassion, which he shows to all who love him and hold on to his mercy. Here is shown certain security. The third is the blessed face as it shall be in eternity. And this was shown most often and at greatest length.

When we are in trouble he shows us the face of his cross and passion, and helps us endure by his own blessed virtue. When we sin his expression is tender and compassionate, and keeps us safe and secure from all our enemies. These two are the normal expressions that we see in this life. Sometimes there is the third, the blessed face of heaven, of which we get a glimpse. And that glimpse comes through his gracious touch and sweet enlightenment in the spiritual life. By it we are safely kept in faith, hope, and charity; in contrition and devotion; and, indeed, in contemplation and every manner of real consolation and comfort. The blessed face of our Lord God effects this result in us by his grace.

Sin in elect souls is temporarily mortal; such souls are not dead in God's sight; here is reason for rejoicing, and sorrow caused by our blindness and the dead weight of our flesh; God's most comforting look; why these revelations were made

72 BUT now I must tell how I saw that mortal sin could be in those who are not going to die because of their sins, but rather are going to live eternally in the joy of God.

I saw that two opposites could never meet anywhere. Of all existing things the most opposite are highest blessedness and deepest pain. The highest blessedness there is, is to have God in the clear light of eternity, seeing him in truth, experiencing his sweetness, and possessing him in utter perfection, and fullest joy. So did the blessed face of our Lord reveal his pity, from which revelation I perceived that sin is of all things most opposed to him; so much so that all the time we tinker with it, however little, we can never see his blessed face clearly. The more horrible and grievous our sins, the further we are, for such time, from that blessed sight. Therefore it often seems to us that we are in deadly peril, and half in hell already, because of the grief and suffering brought to us by sin. So, for the time being, we are dead to the very sight of our blessed life. But at the same time I saw that it is true that in God's sight we are not dead, and that moreover he never leaves us. But he will not have perfect pleasure in us until we find our perfect pleasure in him, seeing his beautiful and blessed face in truth. This is why we have been born, and what we achieve by grace. This is how I saw that sin is only mortal for a short while in those who are blessed with eternal life.

The more clearly the soul sees the blessed face by grace and love, the more it longs to see it in its fullness. Notwithstanding that our Lord God lives in us, and is here with us; notwithstanding that he clasps and enfolds us in his tender love, never to leave us; notwithstanding that he is nearer to us than tongue and heart can think or tell, the fact remains that we shall never cease from sighs, complaints, or tears – or longing – till we see clearly his blessed face. In that precious, blessed sight, no grief can live, no blessing fail.

In this I saw reason for cheer, and reason for sighing; cheer, in that our Lord and Maker is so near us; he is in us, and we are in him, completely safe through his great goodness; sighing, in that we are so spiritually blind and weighed down by our mortal flesh and murky sin that we cannot clearly see our Lord's blessed face. No, and because of this murkiness we have difficulty in believing and trusting his great love and our complete safety. And therefore I say that we never cease from sighs or tears. *Tears* do not mean physical tears of the eye only, but also the inner weeping of the spirit. For the natural desire of the soul is so vast and immeasurable that were we to be given for our comfort and solace all the finest that God has made in heaven and earth, but could not see the beautiful and blessed face of himself, our sighs and spiritual tears and painful longing would never cease until we saw the blessed countenance of our Maker. On the other hand, were we to be in the utmost pain that tongue and heart can think or tell, if then we could see his blessed face, none of this pain would distress us.

So it is that the Beatific Vision is the end of every pain to the loving soul, and the fulfilment of every joy and blessing. And he showed this to be so in those marvellous words, 'It is I who am most exalted; it is I who am most lowly; it is I who am all.' There are three kinds of knowledge as far as we are concerned: (i) that we know our Lord God; (ii) that we know ourselves: what we are by nature and by grace; and (iii) that we know in all humility what our self has become because of our sin and weakness. It was for these three reasons, I believe, that this revelation was made.

The threefold manner of these revelations concerning two kinds of spiritual sickness that God wants us to remedy; we are to remember his passion, and to know that he is all love; we are to be confident and to rejoice in love, and not to be unduly despondent over our past sins.

73 ALL this blessed teaching of our Lord was shown in three ways: by physical sight, by words formed in my intellect, and by spiritual sight. With regard to the physical sight I have related what I have seen as truthfully as I can. For the words I have repeated them exactly as our Lord showed

them me. About the spiritual sight I have already said a fair amount, but I can never describe it fully. So I am prompted to say more about it, if God will give me grace.

God showed two kinds of spiritual sickness that we have: the first is impatience or sloth, for we make such heavy weather of our hardships and suffering; the second is despair or a dread that doubts, of which I am about to speak. He showed me, first, sin in general, in which all sins are included, and then these two in particular. They are the two that most exercise and disturb us, as our Lord showed me. His will is that we should be cured of them. (I am thinking, of course, of those men and women who hate sin because they love God, and who set themselves to do God's will.) Through our spiritual blindness, then, and physical inertia we are most inclined to these two sins. So God wills us to know of them, that we may refuse them as we do other sins.

To help us in this our Lord in his great humility showed us the patience he displayed in his grievous passion, and the joy, too, and delight that such love brought him at the same time. In this he showed himself our example, so that we should endure our suffering gladly and wisely. This gives him much pleasure, and is to our eternal benefit. The reason why we are so exercised with these things is that we are so ignorant of love. Though the Three Persons of the Trinity are all essentially equal, my soul most readily understood love. Yes, it is his will that we see and enjoy everything in love. And it is in our ignorance of this that we are most blind. Some of us believe that God is almighty, and *may* do everything; and that he is all wise, and *can* do everything; but that he is all love, and will do everything – there we draw back. And as I see it, this ignorance is the greatest of all hindrances to God's lovers.

When we begin to hate sin, and to mend our ways under the direction of Holy Church, there still remains within us a dread that holds us back, because we look at ourselves and the sins we have already committed. For some of us it is because we sin every day. We do not keep our promises, or the cleansing our Lord has bestowed upon us, but fall so often into wretchedness shameful to behold. And the sight of this makes us so sorry and despondent that we can scarcely find any comfort. This dread we sometimes mistake for humility, but this is to be horribly blind and weak. We cannot despise it as we do any other sin that we know, for it comes from the enemy, and is opposed to truth. It is the will of God that of all the qualities of the blessed Trinity that we should be most sure of, and delighted with, is love. Love makes might and wisdom come down to our level. For just as by his courtesy God forgives our sin when we repent, so he wills that we forgive our sin too, and as a consequence our foolish despondency and doubting fears.

Dread can take four forms; dread born of reverence is a loving and true dread; humble love always goes with it, yet dread and love are not the same; how we are to pray God for them

74 I BELIEVE dread can take four forms. One is the dread of fright that comes upon a man suddenly because he is weak. This kind does good, for it helps to purge a man as it were, just as physical sickness does, or any other pain that is not sinful. All such suffering helps a man if he takes it patiently. The second is the dread of pain, which will stir and waken a man from the sleep of sin. He will not be able to know the gentle strength of the Holy Spirit until such time as he understands what is meant by this dread of pain, of physical death, of spiritual enemies. It impels us to seek God's strength and mercy; and so God helps us by enabling us to be sorry for our sins through the blessed touch of the Holy Spirit. The third is the dread which doubts. These doubts which tend towards

despair God will have turned into love through our knowledge of his love. In other words, the bitterness of doubt is turned into sweet and kindly love by grace. It never pleases our Lord that his servants should doubt his goodness! The fourth is the dread born of reverence. No dread but this really pleases God. It is so gentle; the greater it is, the less it is felt because its love is correspondingly sweeter.

Love and dread are brothers. They are rooted in us by the goodness of our Maker, and they will never be taken from us. We love by nature, and we love, too, by grace. We dread by nature, and again, we dread by grace. It is right for the lordship and fatherhood of God to be feared, just as it is right for his goodness to be loved. And it is right for us, his servants and his children, to fear his lordship and his fatherhood, just as it is right for us to love him for his goodness. Though this reverent dread and love may not be separated, they are not one but distinct, both in essence and in function. Yet neither can be had without the other. Hence my conviction that he who loves also dreads, even though he may be little aware of it.

All forms of dread other than the reverent one are not really holy though they sometimes seem to be. We can distinguish them in this way: the dread which makes us fly to our Lord from all that is not good (the child to his Mother's bosom!), and fly with our whole heart; the same dread which knows our weakness and our need, and which knows too his everlasting, blessed love and goodness; the dread which finds its salvation in him alone, and clings to him in sure trust – the dread which does all that for us is kind and gracious, good and true. Anything contrary will be wrong, either wholly or in part. The solution is to recognize both states, and to reject the wrong one.

The effects which in this life naturally stem from reverent dread become, through the gracious working of the Holy

Spirit, in heaven and before God, gentle, courteous, and delightful. There, through our love for him, we shall be near God and really at home; at the same time, through our dread, we shall be gentle before him, and courteous. Love and dread are both one in the end. It is our desire to fear our Lord God with all reverence, to love him in all humility, and to trust him with all our strength. When we dread and love him thus our trust is never in vain. The more we trust, and the more its strength, the more we please and honour the Lord we trust in. If we fail in this reverent dread and humble love (which God forbid!) our trust will be adversely affected at the same time. So there is much need to pray for grace from our Lord that he may give us this reverent dread and humble love both in our heart and in our work. For without this no one can please God.

We have need of love, longing, and pity; God's longing takes three forms, and so does ours; on the Day of Judgement the joy of the blessed will be increased as they see the true reason for all that God has done; they will tremble and fear, rejoice and be thankful; they will marvel at the greatness of God, the completion of his creation

75 I saw that God can supply all our needs. There are three things that I would say we need: love, longing, and pity – the pity of love to protect us in our time of need, and the longing of the same love to draw us up to heaven. For the thirst of God is to include Everyman within himself, and it is through this thirst that he has drawn his holy ones into their present blessedness. He is ever drawing and drinking, as it were, as he gets these living members, yet he still thirsts and longs.

I saw that God's longing takes three forms but all have the

same object. (The same is true of us too, in the matter of long-ing and object alike.) The first is his longing to teach us to know and love him more and more – which both suits and helps us. The second is his longing to have us share in his blessedness, like souls who have been taken out of suffering into heaven. The third is to fill us full of bliss – this will happen on the Last Day, when we shall be filled full to everlasting. For I saw (as I knew already by our Faith) that there will be an end to pain and sorrow for those to be saved. And we shall re-ceive not only the same bliss that souls in heaven already know, but a new one in addition, which will flow in abundance from God and fill us to the brim. These are the good things that he has planned to give us from the very first. They are now stored and hidden within himself, for till that time comes no creature is fit enough or capable of receiving them.

In this fulfilment we shall see the true reason why God has done all the things he has, and the reason, too, for all those things he has permitted. The bliss and the fulfilment will be so vast in its immensity that the whole creation, wondering and astonished, will have for God a dread so great and reverent and beyond anything known before, that the very pillars of heaven will tremble and quake! But there will be no pain in this trembling and dread; it is wholly right that the worth and majesty of God should thus be seen by his creatures, who tremble in dread and quake in humble joy, as they marvel at the greatness of God their Maker, and the insignificance of all that is made. The consideration of all this makes the creature wonderfully meek and mild!

Therefore God wills what in fact we already know by nature and grace: that we should understand and appreciate all this, and so want to work for its realization. This will lead us the right way, keep us in true life, and unite us to God. God is as good as he is great; and if it is right that his goodness should be loved, it is also right that his greatness should be feared. This reverent dread is the 'fair courtesy' of heaven before the face of God. Just as he will be known and loved much beyond anything experienced now, so too will he be feared. All heaven and earth inevitably tremble and quake when the pillars do so!

The loving soul hates the vileness of sin more than all the pains of hell; the consideration of other men's sins, unless it is done with compassion, hinders our contemplation of God; the Devil, by reminding us of our wretchedness, would hinder us thus, and by our sloth as well

76 I AM not saying much about this reverent dread, because I hope it will be clear enough from what has been said already. I am quite sure of this: our Lord showed me no souls who did not dread him. For I am just as sure that a soul who genuinely accepts the teaching of the Holy Spirit hates sin for its vileness and horror even more than it hates the pains of hell. A soul who has seen the loving kindness of our Lord Jesus will hate not hell but sin – or so it seems to me. Therefore it is God's will that we know about sin: and so as not to fall blindly into it, that we should pray earnestly, work willingly, and seek humbly such teaching as will help us. Should we fall, we are to get up at once. The most painful thing a soul can do is to turn from God through sin.

The soul that would preserve its peace, when another's sin is brought to mind, must fly from it as from the pains of hell, looking to God for help against it. To consider the sins of other people will produce a thick film over the eyes of our soul, and prevent us for the time being from seeing the 'fair beauty of the Lord' – unless, that is, we look at them contrite along with the sinner, being sorry with and for him, and yearning over him for God. Without this it can only harm, disturb, and hinder the soul who considers them. I gathered all this from the revelation about compassion.

In this blessed revelation of our Lord I begin to understand two very different things: the greatest wisdom a man can attain in this life, and the greatest folly. The greatest wisdom is to fulfil the will and plan of his most exalted Friend. This blessed Friend is Jesus; it is his will and plan that we hang on to him, and hold tight always, in whatever circumstances; for whether we are filthy or clean is all the same to his love. He wants us never to run away from him, whether things are going well or ill. But because our self is so changeable we often fall into sin. And then we are influenced by our enemy and our own blind folly. 'See,' they say. 'You are a wretched creature, a sinner, and a liar to boot. You do not keep God's commandments. You are always promising our Lord to do better, and then you immediately go and fall again into the same sin – and particularly into sloth, and time wasting.' It looks to me as though sin begins here, especially in the case of those who have given themselves to serve our Lord contemplatively, gazing at his blessed goodness. And this makes us dread appearing before our courteous Lord. Thus would our enemy set us back with this false dread of our wretchedness, and the pain he threatens us with. He means to make us so despondent and weary that we forget all about the lovely, blessed sight of our everlasting Friend.

The enmity of the Fiend, who loses more by our getting up again than he gains by our falling; therefore he is despised; God's chastening can be borne by remembering his passion; this brings a greater reward than does our chosen penance; suffering is inevitable, but our courteous God is our leader, keeper, and blessedness

77 Our good Lord showed me the enmity of the Fiend, from which I gathered that everything opposed to love and peace comes from the Fiend and his set. Inevitably we fall because of our weakness and stupidity – and just as surely as we get up with even greater joy because of the mercy and grace of the Holy Spirit. Even if our enemy gains something from us when we fall (this is what he likes!), he loses very much more because of our love and humility when we get up again. This glorious rising up gives him such sorrow and pain (he hates our soul so much) that he burns and burns with envy. The very sorrow he would impose on us turns back upon himself. Which was the reason why our Lord spurned him – and the reason, too, why I laughed so much.

The remedy is to be aware of our wretchedness, and to fly to our Lord. The greater our need, the more important it is to draw near to him. Let our meaning be, 'I am well aware that my suffering is deserved. Our Lord is almighty, and may punish me mightily; he is all-wise, and can punish me wisely; and he is all-good, and loves me most tenderly.' And with the sight of this we have got to stay. The humility of a sinful soul is a lovely thing, and is a work of the Spirit's mercy and grace, when we consciously and gladly accept the scourge and punishment given by our Lord himself. It even becomes gentle and bearable when we are really content with him and with what he does. What penance a man should impose upon himself was not revealed to me – not specifically at any rate. But this was shown, with particular and loving emphasis, that we are to accept and endure humbly whatever penance God himself gives us, with his blessed passion ever in mind. When in pitying love we recall his blessed passion we suffer with him, as did his friends who actually saw it. This was shown in the thirteenth revelation, near the beginning, where it speaks of pity. For he says, 'Do not accuse yourself too much, nor think that your distress and grief is all your fault. It is not my purpose that you should be unreasonably depressed or sorrowful. You will experience distress whatever you do. Therefore I want you to understand your penance, and to recognize that your whole life itself is a profitable penance.' This place is a prison, and this life a penance. In remedying it he wants us to rejoice. The remedy is the fact that our Lord is with us, protecting us and leading us into fullness of joy. For it is an unending source of joy to us that our Lord should intend that he, our protector here, is to be our bliss there – our way and our heaven is true love and sure trust! This is the message of all the revelations, and particularly in that of his passion where he made me wholeheartedly choose him to be my heaven.

Flee to our Lord and we shall be strengthened. Touch him, and we shall be cleansed. Cling to him, and we shall be safe and sound from every danger. For it is the will of our courteous Lord that we should be as much at home with him as heart may think or soul desire. But we must be careful not to accept this privilege so casually that we forget our own courtesy. For our Lord himself is supremely friendly, and he is as courteous as he is friendly: he is very courteous. And he will have his blessed ones in heaven like himself in all respects. To be perfectly like our Lord is true salvation indeed, and utter bliss. If we do not know how to manage this, let us ask our Lord to teach us. For this is what he likes, and it honours him. Bless him!

Our Lord wants us to know that his goodness takes four forms; we need the light of grace to know our sin and weakness; we have nothing but wretchedness; we cannot know the ghastliness of sin itself; our enemy wishes to prevent us from knowing our sin until the very end; we are much indebted to God for showing it now

78 In his merciful way our Lord shows us our sin and weakness by that light, lovely and gracious, which shines from himself. Our sin is so vile and horrible that in his courtesy he will not show it us except under the light of his mercy and grace. It is his will that we should know four things: (i) that he is the ground of our life and existence; (ii) that he protects us by his might and mercy all the time we are in sin among the enemies out to wreck us – we are in so much the greater danger since we give them the opportunity they want, being ignorant of our own need; (iii) how courteously he protects us, making us know when we are going astray; (iv) how loyally he waits for us, with unvarying affection: he wants us to turn to him, uniting with him in love, as he is with us.

So it is that with this gracious information we are able to view our sin positively and not despairingly. For, indeed, we must face it and by such sight be made ashamed of ourselves, and humbled for our pride and presumption. We have got to see that of ourselves we are nothing but sin and wretchedness. We can estimate from the little our Lord shows us how great is the total we do not see. For in his courtesy he limits the amount we actually see: we could not stand the sight of what in fact it is, so vile and horrible is it. And by this humiliating knowledge, through our contrition and his grace we shall break with everything that is not our Lord. Then will our blessed Saviour heal us completely, and unite us to himself.

This break—and healing our Lord intends for mankind generally. The man who is highest and nearest to God sees himself as sinful and as needy as I am; and I who am the least and most lowly of all who are to be saved can be comforted along with the highest. So has our Lord made us one in his charity.

When he showed me that I should sin, I was so enjoying looking at him that I did not pay much attention to this revelation, so our Lord in his courtesy refrained from further teaching until he gave me the grace and will to attend. By this I was taught that though we may be raised to contemplation by our Lord's especial favour we still need to recognize our sin and weakness. Without such knowledge we cannot be truly humble, nor indeed can we be saved.

I saw afterwards, too, that we may not always have this knowledge of ourselves, or of our spiritual enemies – they do not wish us so much good! If they had their way we should not know it till our dying day. We are greatly indebted to God then that he himself, for love's sake, wills to show it to us in this time of mercy and grace.

We are taught about our sin, and not about that of our neighbours, unless it helps; God wants us to realize that any reaction against this view comes from our enemy; because we know the great love of God we are not to get careless about falling; if we do not get up at once after we have fallen we are most unkind to God

79 I UNDERSTOOD more what he meant when he showed me that I should sin. I had taken it simply to refer to me as an individual, nor was the contrary shown me at the time. But by our Lord's very gracious enlightenment

that came subsequently I saw that he meant mankind in general: that is to say, Everyman, who is and will be sinful to the very end. I am included in that man, I hope, by the mercy of God. The blessed comfort that I saw is large enough to embrace us all. This taught me to look at my own sin and not at other men's unless it was going to be a comfort and help to my fellow Christians. In the same revelation about my sinning I learned to be afraid because of my instability. For I do not know in what way I shall fall, nor the extent or greatness of my sin. I would have liked to have known that – with due fear, of course. But I got no answer.

At the same time our courteous Lord showed very clearly and convincingly the eternal and unchanging nature of his love, and that, through the keeping power of his great goodness and grace, there will be no separation between his love and our souls. So in this fear I have good reason for a humility which will save me from presuming, and in that blessed revelation of love good reason too for real and joyful comfort which will keep me from despairing.

This revelation, so intimate and homely, teaches a lovely lesson, and one that is gracious and sweet. It is a comfort for our soul, and comes from our courteous Lord himself. Through his delightful and intimate love he intends us to know that all the experience contrary to this, whether it be within us, or without, is from the enemy and not from God. For example, if we are inclined to get careless about the way we are living or are guarding our hearts because we know this abundant love, there is all the more need for us to beware. This inclination, should it come, is false, and we ought to abominate it. It bears no resemblance to God's will.

When we fall through our weakness or blindness our Lord in his courtesy puts his hand on us, encourages us, and holds on to us. Only then does he will that we should see our wretchedness, and humbly acknowledge it. It is not his intention for us to remain like this, nor that we should go to great lengths in our self-accusation, nor that we should feel too wretched about ourselves. He means us to look at once to him. For he stands there apart, waiting for us to come in sorrow and grief. He is quick to receive us, for we are his delight and joy, and he our salvation and our life. (When I say he is 'standing apart', I am not thinking of the blessed company of heaven, but am speaking of his office and work here on earth – which are the circumstances of the revelation.)

By three things is God worshipped, and we are saved; our present knowledge is but the ABC; our sweet Jesus does it all; he abides with us; and grieves for us; when we sin only he grieves; then it is for us to turn back to him at once, out of kindness and reverence

80 IN this life man is able to stand because of three things; by these same things God is worshipped, and we are helped, kept, and saved. The first is the use of man's natural reason; the second, the everyday teaching of Holy Church; the third, the inner working of grace through the Holy Spirit. All three come from the one God. God is the source of our natural reason; God the basis of the teaching of Holy Church; and God is the Holy Spirit. Each is a distinct gift which we are meant to treasure and to heed. All of them are continually at work in us leading us Godwards. These are great things, and God's will is that we should know something about them here below: to know the ABC as it were, and have the full understanding in heaven. All this will help us on our way.

We know by our Faith that God alone – and no one else – took our nature; moreover, that Christ alone – and no one else – has done all that is necessary for our salvation. In the same way he alone brings it to its final end. In other words, it is he who dwells with us here, who rules and governs us in this life, and who brings us to his blessedness. And this he will do all the while there is any soul on earth destined for heaven. So much so, that if there were only one such soul, he would be with that one soul, alone, till he had brought him to bliss. I believe and understand what the clergy tell me about the ministrations of angels, but nothing was shown me of this. But he himself is nearest us, and the most humble; highest and the most lowly; he does it all. And not only all that we need, but every splendid thing is done by him – to our great joy in heaven. And when I saw that he waits for us in sorrow and grief, it involves us in a genuine contrition and compassion, a sorrowing and grieving that we are not yet one with our Lord. Every such-like thing that helps us is due to Christ in us. And though some of us feel it seldom, it never leaves Christ until he has brought us out of our trouble. We cannot love and not pity. When we fall, and forget all about him and the need for guarding our soul, then Christ alone accepts the responsibility, and so he stands in sorrow and grief.

Then it is only reverent and kind for us to turn quickly to our Lord, and not leave him on his own. He is here alone with us all. That is to say, he is only here for our sakes. And whenever I estrange myself from him by sin or despair or sloth, then I let my Lord stand alone so far as I am concerned. And so it is with all sinners. But though we behave like this so often, his goodness never allows us to be on our own: he is always with us, and in his merciful way he makes excuses for us, and shields us from any blame.

The blessed woman saw God in many ways, but she saw him take his rest nowhere but in man's soul; his will is that we rejoice more in his love than we sorrow over our frequent falls, that we remember the everlasting reward, and live in glad penitence; why God allows sin

81 OUR good Lord showed himself to me in various ways both in heaven and on earth. But the only *place* I saw him occupy was in man's soul. He showed himself on earth in his precious incarnation and his blessed passion. In another way he showed himself – on earth still – when I said 'I saw the whole Godhead as it were in a single point.' Yet another way was his showing of himself as being as it were on pilgrimage; in other words, he is here with us, leading us on, and staying by us until he has brought us all to his blessedness in heaven. He often showed himself as reigning, as I have related, but chiefly in man's soul. There he has made his resting place, and his glorious city. From this most honoured abode he will never rise nor remove.

The place of the Lord's dwelling is wonderful and splendid, so he wants us to respond at once to his gracious touch, rejoicing in the completeness of his love rather than sorrowing over our frequent falls. Of all the things we may do for him in our penitence the most honouring to him is to live gladly and gaily because of his love. So mercifully does he look on us that he regards our whole life here as a penance. That deep longing we have for him is a never ending penance to us: it is a penance that he produces in us, and one which he mercifully helps us to bear. His love makes him long for us; his wisdom, truth, and righteousness enable him to tolerate our being here; and he wants us to see it this way too. This is a very kind penance, in my view, and the greatest! It will be with us until such time as we are made perfect, when we shall possess him as our reward. And so he wills that we set our heart on that 'pass-over' – over from the pain we now experience into the bliss we trust in.

God looks at the soul's grief with pity, not blame; yet we do nothing but sin; in it we are kept in solace and fear; God wants us to turn to him, and cling to his love, and see him to be our medicine; we must love, in longing and enjoyment; anything opposed to this comes from the enemy, not God

82 But here our courteous Lord showed me our soul mourning and moaning. He explained, 'I know very well that your will is to live loving me, enduring cheerfully and gladly whatever penance may come. But since you do not live without sinning, you are willing to suffer, for love of me, all the distress, trouble, and discomfort that may come. Rightly so. But do not be too perturbed by the sins you commit involuntarily.'

Here I came to understand how the Lord looks at his servant with pity, and not with censure. This passing life does not ask us to live altogether without blame or sin. He loves us eternally – and we sin constantly! He shows us our sin so quietly, and then we are sorry and mourn over each one; we turn to see his mercy, and cling to his love and goodness, for we realize that he is our medicine while we do nothing but sin. So, humbled by the sight of our sin, and knowing and trusting his love, we thank him and praise him and please him. 'I love you, and you love me,' he has said, 'and our love will never be broken. For your sake I suffer these things.' All this was shown to my spirit's understanding when these blessed words were said, 'I will keep you safe and sound.'

By the great desire I have in our blessed Lord that we should live in this way – longing and rejoicing, as this lesson on love shows – I understood that all impediments come not from him but from the enemy. He wills us to know this through the gracious and sweet light of his kindly love. Should there be anywhere one of his lovers who is forever kept from falling I know nothing about it: it was not shown me. But this was shown: both when we fall and when we get up again we are kept in the same precious love. In God's sight we do not fall: in our own we do not stand. I see both of these to be true. But God's sight is the higher truth. We are deeply indebted to him that he should want to show us this great truth here below. I saw that it is a very great help for us to see both these truths at one and the same time while we are alive here. The higher, 'God's sight', comforts us spiritually in him, and gives us true enjoyment; the other, more lowly, sight keeps us fearful and ashamed. But our good Lord wants us always to pay more attention to the higher, while not neglecting all knowledge of the lower, until the time we are brought to heaven, where our reward will be the Lord Jesus, and we shall be filled with joy and bliss for ever.

Three attributes of God: life, love, and light; our reason agrees; it is God's greatest gift; our faith is a light which comes from the Father; it is measured to our need, and leads us through the night; at the end of our troubles our eyes will be opened suddenly; this full light and clarity is God our Maker, Father, and Holy Spirit, through Jesus, our Saviour

83 I HAD, in some measure, both touch, sight, and feeling of three of God's attributes, and on them the strength and effectiveness of the whole revelation depends. They occur in every revelation, and particularly in the twelfth where it is often said, 'It is I.' The attributes are these: life, love, and light.

In 'life' there is this marvellous intimacy, and in 'love' that gentle courtesy, and in 'light' our everlasting nature. These three exist in one goodness; to which goodness my own reason would be united, holding on to it with all its power. I gazed with reverence and fear, greatly wondering both at the sight itself and at the feeling of sweet harmony that our reason should be in God. I knew it was the greatest gift we have ever received, and one that was based in our nature.

Our faith is a light, coming to us naturally from him who is our everlasting Day, our Father, and our God. By this light Christ, our Mother, and the Holy Spirit, our good Lord, lead us through these passing years. The light is measured to our individual needs as we face our night. Because of the light we live: because of the night we suffer and grieve. Through this grief we earn reward and thanks from God! With the help of mercy and grace, we know and trust our light quite deliberately, and with it we go forward intelligently and firmly. When we are done with grief our eyes will be suddenly enlightened, and in the shining brightness of the light we shall see perfectly. For our light is none other than God our Maker, and the Holy Spirit, in our Saviour, Christ Jesus.

So did I see and understand that faith is our light in darkness, and our light is God, the everlasting Day.

This light is charity; it is not so insignificant as not to be needed; we are to strive to deserve the eternal and glorious gratitude of God; faith and hope lead us to charity, and its three modes

84 THIS light is charity, and by the wisdom of God it is measured so as to give us full benefit. It is not so bright that we can see now the day of our blessedness, but on

the other hand it is not hidden from us. It is a light such as we can live in profitably, and in which we may strive to deserve the everlasting glory of God. This was shown in the sixth revelation where it was said, 'Thank you for your service and all your suffering.'

So charity keeps us in faith and hope, and hope leads us on in charity. In the end it will be all charity. I understood this light of charity in three ways: (i) charity as uncreated; (ii) charity as created; and (iii) charity as given. 'Uncreated charity' is God; 'created charity' is our soul in God; 'given charity' is virtue. It is a gracious gift, and it works in us so that we love God for himself, and love ourselves in God, and love what God loves, for his sake.

God loved his elect from all time; he never allows them to be hurt so that their bliss is lessened; secrets now hidden in heaven will be known; we shall bless our Lord that everything is so well ordered

85 AT the sight of this I marvelled greatly. Notwithstanding our foolishness and blindness here below, our courteous Lord always has regard for us, rejoicing at this work in our souls. We please him best of all by believing this intelligently and honestly, and rejoicing over it with him and in him. Just as we shall partake of God's blessedness for ever, praising him and thanking him, so have we existed in God's foreknowledge, loved and known in his eternal purpose, from all time. In his timeless love he made us, and in the same love keeps us, never allowing us to be hurt in such a way that our blessedness be lost. Therefore when Judgement is pronounced and we are all brought up to heaven, we shall see clearly in God secrets that are now hidden from us. None of us will want to say then, 'Lord, if only it had happened in this way or that

it would have been perfectly all right.' Rather we will exclaim with one voice, 'Lord, you are blessed indeed! So it is, and it is good! Now we can truly see that everything has been done as it was ordained before creation.'

The good Lord showed that this book should be written differently from the first attempt; he wants us to pray thus for his work: thanking, trusting, and enjoying him; he gave this revelation because he wants it to be known; in such knowledge he will give us grace to love him; after fifteen years the answer was given: the reason for this whole revelation was love. May Jesus grant us this love! Amen

86 THIS book was begun by the gift and grace of God. I do not think it is done yet. We all need to pray God for charity. God is working in us, helping us to thank and trust and enjoy him. Thus does our good Lord will that we should pray. This is what I understood his meaning to be throughout, and in particular when he uttered those sweet, cheering words, 'I am the foundation of your praying.' I knew truly that the reason why our Lord showed it was that he wants it to be better known than it is. It is by our knowing this that he gives us grace to love and to hold to him. He regards his heavenly treasure on earth with so much love that he wants us to have all the greater light and consolation in the joys of heaven. So he draws our hearts away from the sorry murk in which they live.

From the time these things were first revealed I had often wanted to know what was our Lord's meaning. It was more than fifteen years after that I was answered in my spirit's understanding. 'You would know our Lord's meaning in this thing? Know it well. Love was his meaning. Who showed it you? Love. What did he show you? Love. Why did he show it? For love. Hold on to this and you will know and understand love more and more. But you will not know or learn anything else – ever!'

So it was that I learned that love was our Lord's meaning. And I saw for certain, both here and elsewhere, that before ever he made us, God loved us; and that his love has never slackened, nor ever shall. In this love all his works have been done, and in this love he has made everything serve us; and in this love our life is everlasting. Our beginning was when we were made, but the love in which he made us never had beginning. In it we have our beginning.

All this we shall see in God for ever. May Jesus grant this. Amen.

POSTSCRIPT BY THE SCRIBE WHO WROTE THIS BOOK FOR JULIAN

So ends the revelation of the love of the blessed Trinity shown in our Saviour, Christ Jesus. It is our everlasting strength and comfort and rejoicing as we pass on our journey through life. Amen, Jesus, Amen.

I pray God almighty that this book shall fall only into the hands of those who intend to be his lovers, and who are willing to submit to the Faith of Holy Church, and to obey such sound and instructive teaching as is given by men of virtue, maturity, and profound learning. For this revelation contains deep theology and great wisdom, and is not meant for those who are enslaved by sin and the Devil.

Beware of selecting only what you like, and leaving the rest. That is what heretics do. Take it whole, all together, and know in truth that all agrees with Holy Scripture, and is, indeed, based on it. And Jesus, our real love, light, and truth, will show this wisdom of his to all souls who, cleansed from their sin, humbly and perseveringly ask him.

And you, in whose hands this book is, should thank our Saviour Jesus Christ with generous and genuine gratitude. For through his endless love, mercy, and goodness, he has given you these revelations to help you and to guide us all safely to his everlasting bliss.

> May Jesus grant this. Amen.

MORE ABOUT PENGUINS
AND PELICANS

For further information about books available from Penguins please write to Dept EP, Penguin Books Ltd, Harmondsworth, Middlesex UB7 0DA.

In the U.S.A.: For a complete list of books available from Penguins in the United States write to Dept CS, Penguin Books, 625 Madison Avenue, New York, New York 10022.

In Canada: For a complete list of books available from Penguins in Canada write to Penguin Books Canada Ltd, 2801 John Street, Markham, Ontario L3R 1B4.

In Australia: For a complete list of books available from Penguins in Australia write to the Marketing Department, Penguin Books Australia Ltd, P.O. Box 257, Ringwood, Victoria 3134.

DANTE

LA VITA NUOVA

TRANSLATED BY BARBARA REYNOLDS

'*La Vita Nuova* is a treatise by a poet, written for poets, on the art of poetry.' This reinterpretation by Barbara Reynolds allows the reader fresh insights into one of the world's greatest romantic poems. As his love for Beatrice develops, Dante (1265–1321) learns to surmount the barriers of medieval poetic convention and to write directly from experience. And in the prose commentary he recalls this experience and describes its transmutation into poetry. This is, in Dr Reynolds's words, 'an invitation by Dante to enter his study and stand beside him while he runs a finger down the parchment page of his manuscript'.

Also available:

THE DIVINE COMEDY

I: HELL
Translated by Dorothy L. Sayers

II: PURGATORY
Translated by Dorothy L. Sayers

III: PARADISE
Translated by Dorothy L. Sayers and Barbara Reynolds

THOMAS À KEMPIS
THE IMITATION OF CHRIST

TRANSLATED BY LEO SHERLEY-PRICE

For over five hundred years *The Imitation of Christ*, Thomas à Kempis's guide towards Christian perfection, has continued to exercise a widespread influence over Christians of every age and race. Unfortunately most English translators have tended to misrepresent this book – either by making alterations in the text to accord with their personal views, or by presenting it in a pseudo-Jacobean style. Thus many would-be readers have missed the advantage of Thomas's profound wisdom, his clarity of thought and vision, his wide knowledge of the Scriptures and Fathers, and his clear understanding of human nature and its needs. It was time for a new translation.

THE CLOUD OF UNKNOWING

TRANSLATED BY
CLIFTON WOLTERS

Like Thomas À Kempis's *The Imitation of Christ*, *The Cloud of Unknowing* springs from an age when European mysticism was in full flower. Its author was probably an English country parson of the late fourteenth century; but his exact identity remains unknown. The book's main theme is that God cannot be apprehended by man's intellect, and that only love can pierce the 'cloud of unknowing' which lies between them. Its charm and serenity have always ensured it a place among the devotional classics of the Church.

'First-rate and loses nothing by its translation into more common usage' – *The Times Educational Supplement*

CHAUCER
THE CANTERBURY TALES

TRANSLATED BY NEVILL COGHILL

The Canterbury Tales stands conspicuous among the great literary achievements of the Middle Ages. Told by a jovial procession of pilgrims – knight, priest, yeoman, miller, or cook – as they ride towards the shrine of Thomas à Becket, they present a picture of a nation taking shape. The tone of this never-resting comedy is, by turns, learned, fantastic, lewd, pious, and ludicrous. 'Here,' as John Dryden said, 'is God's plenty!'

Geoffrey Chaucer began his great task in about 1386. This version in modern English, by Nevill Coghill, preserves the freshness and racy vitality of Chaucer's narrative.

Also available:
TROILUS AND CRISEYDE

BEDE

A HISTORY OF THE
ENGLISH CHURCH AND PEOPLE

TRANSLATED BY LEO SHERLEY-PRICE

This wonderfully alive tapestry of Saxon England and Celtic Britain written in A.D. 731 still has the power to transport us back to the forests, fens, and mountains, and to the problems which men faced during these crucially formative years when this land had still to be wrought into one entity. Leo Sherley-Price has well succeeded in his aim of producing an accurate and readable version of Bede's work in modern English and, as he remarks in his introduction, 'we realize even more clearly that the past is not dead and done with, but a force to be reckoned with, silently moulding the present and the future'.

THE APOSTOLIC FATHERS
EARLY CHRISTIAN WRITINGS

TRANSLATED BY MAXWELL STANIFORTH

These writings, newly translated from the Greek, are the earliest and most venerable examples of the mass of ecclesiastical literature produced in the first centuries A.D. They are the work of a group known as the Apostolic Fathers, who faithfully preserved the apostolic teaching and tradition between the time of the apostles and the late second century. Most of their writings take the form of epistles: those of Clement of Rome, Ignatius of Antioch and Polycarp, for example, are warmly human and affectionate, while the anonymous *Epistle to Diognetus* and the *Epistle of Barnabas* are more impersonal. All, however, have a genuine pastoral concern – they are interested more in people than in ideas, in practice more than dogma.

SAINT AUGUSTINE
CONFESSIONS

TRANSLATED BY R. S. PINE-COFFIN

Saint Augustine of Hippo (A.D. 354–430) was one of the outstanding figures of the declining Roman Empire. From his own account he lived a life of sin until his conversion to Christianity at the age of thirty-two. Twelve years later he gave a personal account of his search for truth in the *Confessions*, where his analysis of the emotional side of Christian experience in the face of sin remains unsurpassed. They are also intensely revealing of the man himself.

Also published
CITY OF GOD
*Translated by Henry Bettenson
and edited by David Knowles*
(A Pelican Classic)

THE PENGUIN CLASSICS

A Selection:

THE PSALMS
Translated by Peter Levi

Balzac
SELECTED SHORT STORIES
Translated by Sylvia Raphael

Flaubert
SALAMMBO
Translated by A.J. Krailsheimer

Zola
LA BÊTE HUMAINE
Translated by Leonard Tancock

A NIETZSCHE READER
Translated by R.J. Hollingdale

Cao Xueqin
**THE STORY OF THE STONE VOLUME TWO:
THE CRAB-FLOWER CLUB**
Translated by David Hawkes

Balzac
THE WILD ASS'S SKIN
Translated by H.J. Hunt

Cicero
LETTERS TO ATTICUS
Translated by D.R. Shackleton Bailey